DEVELOPING MOTOR AND SOCIAL SKILLS

DEVELOPING MOTOR AND SOCIAL SKILLS

ACTIVITIES FOR CHILDREN WITH AUTISM SPECTRUM DISORDER

Chris Denning

ROWMAN & LITTLEFIELD
Lanham • Boulder • New York • London

Published by Rowman & Littlefield
A wholly owned subsidiary of
The Rowman & Littlefield Publishing Group, Inc.
4501 Forbes Boulevard, Suite 200, Lanham, Maryland 20706
www.rowman.com

Unit A, Whitacre Mews, 26-34 Stannary Street, London SE11 4AB

British Library Cataloguing in Publication Information Available

Library of Congress Cataloging-in-Publication Data

Names: Denning, Christopher, 1972- author.
Title: Developing motor and social skills : activities for children with autism spectrum disorder / Christopher Denning.
Description: Lanham : Rowman & Littlefield, [2017] | Includes bibliographical references.
Identifiers: LCCN 2017003342 (print) | LCCN 2017017229 (ebook) | ISBN 9781475817669 (electronic) | ISBN 9781475817645 (cloth : alk. paper) | ISBN 9781475817652 (pbk. : alk. paper)
Subjects: LCSH: Physical education for children with disabilities. | Autistic children—Education. | Perceptual-motor learning.
Classification: LCC GV445 (ebook) | LCC GV445 .D46 2017 (print) | DDC 371.9/04486—dc23
LC record available at https://lccn.loc.gov/2017003342

∞™ The paper used in this publication meets the minimum requirements of American National Standard for Information Sciences—Permanence of Paper for Printed Library Materials, ANSI/NISO Z39.48-1992.

Printed in the United States of America

To teachers and their students. I hope this book provides ideas that will bring lots of positive energy to your school day.

CONTENTS

FIGURES

TABLES AND TEXTBOXES

TABLES

TEXTBOXES

PREFACE

Educators work with children placed in a variety of school environments. Although recent research (e.g., Kurth, 2014) indicates that the majority of children with an autism spectrum disorder (ASD) are educated in inclusive settings, the 2004 Individuals with Disabilities Education Act (IDEA) mandates that individualized education program (IEP) teams consider a continuum of placement options based on the child's needs.

Regardless of the severity of the disability, including language and motor development, physical activity programs can be successfully implemented (see, e.g., Lang et al., 2010). I base this statement on both a growing body of research demonstrating positive effects from motor skill activities and exercise, and over 15 years of experience working with young children with ASD as a classroom teacher, consultant, and researcher. To ensure success, however, children with more intensive needs will need additional support.

The classroom can be a challenging place for kids with ASD for multiple reasons. The environment frequently feels chaotic for them, and is often filled with roadblocks and detours throughout the day. As I look back on my years working with children with ASD across a variety of schools and settings, I can see the common thread that physical activity and motor development held in my students' success.

When I started teaching, we took breaks every 30–45 minutes throughout the day. These breaks occurred within the classroom, in the hallway, outside, in the school gymnasium, or anywhere we could find space for activities such as running, swinging, jumping, and playing catch. My intention was twofold: to break up the school day, and to help students regain focus. The kids had fun doing it. I could also see that these breaks worked by helping students refocus and by reducing behaviors like self-stimulation, but I had no idea of the impact of physical activity based on what we know today.

I have conducted research with early childhood teachers to implement motor development programs that incorporate physical activity. We've seen positive changes in motor development, social interactions, and appropriate behaviors. More importantly, both students and teachers enjoy doing it. This book will outline what we now know about how physical activity impacts children with ASD, and how teachers can use physical activity programs in their classrooms.

REFERENCES

Kurth, J. (2014). Educational placement of students with ASD: The impact of state of residence. *Focus on Autism and Developmental Disabilities, 30*(4), 1–8. doi:10.1177/1088357614547891

Lang, R., Koegel, L. K., Ashbaugh, K., Regester, A., Ence, W., & Smith, W. (2010). Physical exercise and individuals with autism spectrum disorders: A systematic review. *Research in Autism Spectrum Disorders, 4*, 565–76.

ACKNOWLEDGMENTS

I'm grateful for the support and dedication of many individuals. My wife, Christine, reviewed multiple drafts of chapters and contributed her expertise in yoga and child development to help with the sections on cool down. My children—Catharine, Alessandra, and Jude—modeled for the motor development figures, and help keep me moving every day.

I would like to thank my colleague, Dr. Rona Flippo, who encouraged me to pursue the book and helped connect me to Rowman & Littlefield. Thanks go to my editor, Dr. Thomas Koerner, and associate editor, Carlie Wall, for their patience as I navigated completion of the book and for their support throughout the process.

I am so impressed with all the teachers I've had the pleasure to work with at the Early Learning Center in Quincy, Massachusetts. They did so much with the children and found ways to embed motor development and physical activity into their school day. I thank the parents for allowing me to work with their children, and both Kerri Connolly and Judy Todd for their patience and support throughout the project that led to this book.

I'd like to thank Dr. Amelia Moody, Erica Ouellette, and Jan LaPrade for sharing their varied expertise with me and spending their time to review chapter drafts. Finally, I thank my nephew, John Flanagan, for drawing the figures depicting motor movements. I've wanted to capture John's talent in a book since he first amazed us all with his art in elementary school (or earlier!). Finally did it.

INTRODUCTION

This book is organized into three main sections. The first section, chapters 1–3, describes the importance of physical activity and the focus on motor development for children with autism spectrum disorder (ASD) based on the current knowledge base. The second section, chapters 4–6, describes a model for developing a classroom program that simultaneously focuses on physical activity, motor development, and social skills. Last, the final chapter outlines how to involve other professionals and families in the classroom physical activity program.

Chapter 1 is set up to help teachers understand the unique challenges that children with ASD experience in the classroom during physical activity programs. Ideas in the chapter focus upon the needs children with ASD might have in the school environment, and the evidence-based strategies that can be used during physical activity programs.

The second chapter highlights recent research on motor development and physical activity, especially the impacts on brain chemistry, brain development, and learning. This is one of the key chapters in the book, and was exciting to research. The intention is to highlight the importance of physical activity for students with ASD and why part of their day should be devoted to this area.

Similarly, chapter 3 examines the connections between physical activity, motor development, and social skills. This is a crucial area for children with ASD as both researchers and practitioners search for ways to support social development. We've seen positive changes in social interactions in the classroom during physical activity programs, and recent research notes these connections as well. The chapter will prepare teachers to learn more about how to support these skills in the next section of the book.

The fourth chapter highlights considerations for teachers as they begin to implement a motor activity program for children with ASD. Key areas in this chapter focus on how the physical activity program should be organized. This includes ways to set up the environment and prepare children for the program. In addition, the chapter focuses on the types of instructional methodologies to use. Setup is often the most crucial part of any program, and this chapter highlights where teachers can focus attention to optimize results.

Chapter 5 explains how to run the physical activity program. Based on my work in schools and reading of recent research, I recommend that a physical activity program contains three key components: (a) physical activity or exercise, (b) motor development activities, and (c) a focused cool down. All three components impact children with ASD, and the rationale for their inclusion is discussed in the chapter.

The chapter also provides many suggestions for ways to include these components flexibly using an à la carte menu. Activities can differ from day to day, or you may find a particular activity that everyone loves and that works well in the classroom environment. If so, great—keep using it. It may be easier to spend 30 minutes a few times a week running a program, or sometimes a teacher can only find 10 minute increments, so shorter segments work better. That's fine too—the chapter highlights ways to run the program in a variety of ways. The chapter concludes with ideas for places to go for additional information.

Chapter 6 highlights key areas for teachers to consider as they support the social development of children with ASD during a physical activity program. This includes selection of target skills and ways to support these skills during the physical activity program. While recent evidence suggests that social skills may improve to some degree just by interacting more with peers during exercise, more is needed at times. Therefore, the chapter provides ways to support specific skills through strategies like targeted grouping, peer supports, or scripts and social narratives.

The final chapter suggests ways to get additional support from knowledgeable colleagues or families. There are multiple benefits from involving families in school programs and collaborating with others in your school, such as adaptive physical education teachers or occupational therapists, who know so much about motor planning and activity.

Good luck as you develop and implement your program. I hope this book can serve as your guide on the journey.

1

UNIQUE ASPECTS OF THE CLASSROOM FOR CHILDREN WITH ASD

WHAT DO CHILDREN WITH ASD NEED TO SUCCEED IN SCHOOL?

Children with autism spectrum disorder (ASD) have a number of unique needs that fall into three general areas: learning, behavior, and social skills. Concerns in each of these areas will affect their ability to successfully engage in a physical activity program. First, these children can have challenges in areas that impact learning, such as figuring out how to work within the classroom environment, accessing new knowledge and material, completing assignments consistently, and keeping motivated (see, e.g., Koegel, Singh, & Koegel, 2010). Additional support and reliance on their strengths, however, can improve performance.

Second, children with ASD can have challenges that impact behavior, such as difficulty with changes in routine, limited flexibility, repetitive patterns of behavior or interests, need for structure, need for predictable routines and procedures, need for consistency, and need for frequent breaks (APA, 2013). As a result, these children tend to thrive on structure, predictable routines and procedures, consistency, and opportunities for movement breaks (see, e.g., Mancil & Pearl, 2008).

Third, they can have challenges that impact their social interactions, such as nonverbal behaviors (e.g., eye gaze, body posture), failure to develop peer relationships, difficulty maintaining conversations, repetitive use of language, being unaware of social conventions, and difficulty with team skills

(APA, 2013). A physical activity program can be part of the way teachers support social growth for children with ASD. These ideas will be outlined in more detail in chapter 3, but it is important to structure the program so children can feel comfortable and have positive outcomes, embed opportunities for social interactions within the program, and teach the skills necessary for children to be successful when these opportunities for interaction arise.

Many strategies can support multiple areas, and proactively planning for these supports can greatly improve the success of children with autism in a physical activity program. Therefore, teachers should plan in advance the environment where the physical activity program is run and the activities that are used so that the students have the best chance for success. Then, work on ways to fine-tune supports in these areas based on the needs of the children.

Research indicates that activity schedules (e.g., Kimball, Kinney, Taylor, & Stromer, 2004), priming (e.g., Gately, 2008), choice (Koegel et al., 2010), special interests (Mancil & Pearl, 2008), routines and procedures (Wong & Wong, 2009), and visual tools (Roberts & Joiner, 2007) can be used during the development and implementation of a school-based program to improve outcomes.

EVIDENCE-BASED STRATEGIES AND SUPPORTS

Evidence suggests that teachers will continue to use supports that can easily fit into their daily classroom routine, are perceived as effective for students, and enrich the teachers' repertoire of instructional methods (Gersten, Chard, & Baker, 2000). With this in mind, I present the following ideas based upon both a body of literature documenting their effectiveness, and evidence from my own experiences as a teacher and consultant. The strategies will also serve as the basis for setting up the environment for physical activity, and developing a routine in the classroom when conducting a physical activity program.

Universal Design for Learning

The first idea is universal design for learning (UDL). Although the evidence base for this practice is limited, it is growing, and it can be effective for many students in a classroom, not just the children the teacher may be focusing on (see, e.g., National Center on Universal Design for Learning, 2009). The intention of UDL "is to create products and/or environments that are designed, from the outset, to accommodate individuals with a wider range of abilities and disabilities than can be accommodated by traditional applications" (Rose, Hasselbring, Stahl, & Zabala, 2005, p. 508).

The three core features of UDL include multiple means of engagement, representation, and expression (Hall, Strangman, & Meyer, 2003). Multiple means of engagement are the hooks that draw students into class activities and spark their imagination. For example, teachers could read a book about animals that hop, and send a copy of the book home. They can also adjust expectations in a physical activity program in order to encourage involvement and create opportunities for success. This feature is typically considered last in UDL, but I think it is crucial for children with ASD. It is so important to gain their interest and capture that attention in an activity.

Multiple means of representation involve ways to present information to more efficiently and effectively support student learning. For example, teachers can demonstrate movements, show videos or pictures, compare movements to animals or star athletes, or use books about movements. Learning may be enhanced when content is made more concrete through visual or hands-on materials (see, e.g., Roberts & Joiner, 2007).

Finally, multiple means of action or expression involve ways that students can effectively demonstrate what they know. For example, students can show what they know in different ways, such as talking about balance or demonstrating when they might need balance (e.g., hitting a baseball, standing on a diving board, jumping on rocks to cross a river). These basic ideas provide ways for structuring activities so that everyone can be more involved.

Visual Supports

Visuals are educational tools used to help individuals with ASD organize information for processing and recall (Roberts & Joiner, 2007). Visual skills are considered to be a relative strength for children with autism, and can be used to support their understanding of the flow of the physical activity program and the performance of specific activities. For example, teachers could use pictures illustrating how to perform specific skills, such as catching the ball or kicking the ball into a goal, or teachers could show a video that demonstrates these skills.

Visual supports provide a concrete representation of what children will do throughout the day. Activity schedules are a type of visual support that provide a representation of what will happen during an activity or school day, and can be beneficial for young children for a number of reasons. They can help children understand the expectations (e.g., Mesibov, Shea, & Schopler, 2005), reduce anxiety, help children prepare for an activity, support transitions, prepare for changes, and support deficits in expressive or receptive language (Kimball et al., 2004).

Teachers can include the physical activity program in the daily schedule, and can even include a mini-schedule that details what will happen during each activity. Another idea is to include a timer that clearly shows how long each activity will last. This could be a stopwatch, a Time Timer, or a digital web-based timer.

Routines and Procedures

Routines are what students do without prompting or supervision, and procedures are how teachers want things done in the classroom (Wong & Wong, 2009). UDL supports for routines and procedures can increase both representation and expression during the school day. Routines and procedures can improve task completion and behavior for students with ASD by providing consistency and clarity for classroom expectations (McIntosh, Herman, Sanford, McGraw, & Florence, 2004).

Teachers need to make procedures explicit by teaching behavioral expectations to students (McIntosh et al., 2004). Procedures should be developed and taught in the same way students are taught academic content or behavioral expectations (Wong & Wong, 2009). First, provide a rationale for the procedure. Next, clearly explain the procedure using a written example of the steps, and demonstrate how each step is completed. Then, practice the procedure with the class multiple times. The goal is mastery.

Finally, monitor the procedure through feedback, reinforcement of attempts, and reteaching when needed. Teachers should create a routine for the physical activity program, so that each day follows the same pattern. You can also create procedures for getting materials, or for putting them away at the end of the activity.

Priming

Priming allows children to know what will happen during an activity by providing access to materials before the activity takes place, or by discussing the details of the event (Koegel, Koegel, Frea, & Green-Hopkins, 2003). Priming can help students with ASD in multiple ways. It can activate prior knowledge, help children create connections with a new activity, and reduce surprises (Gately, 2008). By increasing the comfort level and familiarity with materials or activities, priming may increase the likelihood of attention, task completion, and appropriate responses (O'Connor & Klein, 2004).

Priming can take place at the beginning of the school day, or it can be used as a way to discuss new activities a few days prior to their occurrence. Materials may also be sent home. Including visual and verbal demonstrations can help children understand the expectations for each activity. Grenier and Yeaton (2011) used priming or previewing as way to prepare children with autism for a physical education class. Strategies included breaking down skills and lessons into chunks, demonstrating critical skills, allowing students to touch and manipulate equipment, and engaging in a question-and-answer session.

These strategies are critical for helping children prepare to engage with the activity and the lesson. Teachers should help prepare children for the physical activity program by discussing what they will do, and sending materials home, if possible.

Choice

Children can be given choices in multiple areas, such as the order of activities, the order of items within activities, and the materials used. Choice can be highly motivating, increase the likelihood of task completion, and reduce disruptions for children with ASD (Koegel et al., 2010). Moses (1998) found that providing young children choices in work assignments increased work completion, improved accuracy, and reduced disruptive behaviors.

Choice can be a powerful tool in a physical activity program to create motivation and get children involved, since teachers have complete flexibility to choose each activity. For example, you could provide children with a choice between two different activities that target the skill of the day (e.g., throwing or hitting a ball).

Special Interests

Teachers can use a student's special interests to create engagement in multiple ways (see, e.g., Mancil & Pearl, 2008). Special interests can be blended naturally into classroom activities either by occasionally individualizing work or by creating opportunities for children to choose some of their own topics.

Baker, Koegel, and Koegel (1998) modified playground games based on children's special interests in order to increase the amount of time children engaged with an activity, and increase their positive affect. Games included an outside tag game on a giant map, and a follow-the-leader game that used a Disney character theme. Results indicated that all children engaged with their peers more frequently and experienced a more positive affect. Behavioral improvements also generalized to non-special interest themed games.

The researchers noted that the children seemed to really enjoy the games, and that the children with ASD were viewed as more socially competent by peers due to their knowledge of the special interest theme (e.g., the child knew the locations of all the states). They hypothesized that results may have been related to the high levels of social play observed following the intervention, and to the generalization to non-special interest themes.

TAKEAWAYS

1. Children with ASD can benefit from a physical activity program in multiple ways through changes in learning, behavior, and social skills.
2. It is important for teachers to consider the relationship between the classroom environment and children with ASD when setting up a physical activity program.
3. Most children with ASD have challenges in the classroom related to academic, behavioral, and social performance. The same evidence-

based practices we use to support their growth in these areas should be embedded into a physical activity program.

REFERENCES

American Psychiatric Association (APA). (2013). *Diagnostic and statistical manual of mental disorders* (5th ed.). Washington, DC: Author.

Baker, M., Koegel, R., & Koegel, L. (1998). Increasing the social behavior of young children with ASD using their obsessive behaviors. *Journal of the Association of Persons with Severe Handicaps, 23*, 300–308.

Gately, S. E. (2008). Facilitating reading comprehension for students on the autism spectrum. *Teaching Exceptional Children, 40*(3), 40–45.

Gersten, R., Chard, D., & Baker, S. (2000). Factors enhancing sustained use of research-based practices. *Journal of Learning Disabilities, 33*, 445–57.

Grenier, M., & Yeaton, P. (2011). Previewing: A successful strategy for students with autism. *Journal of Physical Education Recreation & Dance, 82*(1), 28–43.

Hall, T., Strangman, N., & Meyer, A. (2003). *Differentiated instruction and implications for UDL implementation.* Wakefield, MA: National Center on Accessing the General Curriculum.

Individuals With Disabilities Education Act (IDEA), 20 U.S.C. § 1400 (2004).

Kimball, J., Kinney, E., Taylor, B., & Stromer, R. (2004). Video enhanced activity schedules for children with ASD: A promising package for teaching social skills. *Education and Treatment of Children, 27*, 280–98.

Koegel, L., Koegel, R. L., Frea, W., & Green-Hopkins, I. (2003). Priming as a method of coordinating educational services for students with ASD. *Language, Speech, and Hearing Services in Schools, 34*(3), 228–35. doi:10.1044/0161-1461(2003/019)

Koegel, L. K., Singh, A. K., & Koegel, R. L. (2010). Improving motivation for academics in children with autism. *Journal of Autism and Developmental Disorders, 40,* 1057–66. doi:10.1007/s10803-010-0962-6

Mancil, G. R., & Pearl, C. E. (2008). Restricted interests as motivators: Improving academic engagement and outcomes of children on the autism spectrum. *Teaching Exceptional Children Plus, 4*(6), Article 7.

McIntosh, K., Herman, K., Sanford, A., McGraw, K., & Florence, K. (2004). Transitions: Techniques for promoting success between lessons. *Teaching Exceptional Children, 37*(1), 32–38.

Mesibov, G., Shea, V., & Schopler, E. (2005). *The TEACCH approach to autism spectrum disorders.* New York: Kluwer Academic/Plenum Publishers.

Moses, D. R. (1998). Integrating choice-making opportunities within teacher-assigned academic tasks to facilitate the performance of children with ASD. *Journal of the Association for Persons with Severe Handicaps, 23*(4), 319–28.

National Center on Universal Design for Learning. (2009). *UDL guidelines, version 2.0: Research evidence.* Retrieved from http://www.udlcenter.org/research/researchevidence/

O'Connor, I. E., & Klein, P. D. (2004). Exploration of strategies for facilitating the reading comprehension of high-functioning students with autism spectrum disorders. *Journal of Autism and Developmental Disorders, 34*(2), 115–27.

Roberts, V., & Joiner, R. (2007). Investigating the efficacy of concept mapping with pupils with autistic spectrum disorder. *British Journal of Special Education, 34,* 127–35.

Rose, D. H., Hasselbring, T. S., Stahl, S., & Zabala, J. (2005). Assistive technology and universal design for learning: Two sides of the same coin. In D. Edyburn, K. Higgins, & R. Boone (Eds.), *Handbook of special education technology research and practice* (pp. 507–18). Whitefish Bay, WI: Knowledge by Design.

Wong, H., & Wong, R. (2009). *How to be an effective teacher: The first days of school.* Mountain View, CA: Wong Publications.

2

WHY DO PHYSICAL ACTIVITY AND MOTOR DEVELOPMENT MATTER?

THE IMPORTANCE OF MOTOR DEVELOPMENT AND PHYSICAL ACTIVITY

Delays in motor development and limited physical activity appear to be linked to health outcomes, such as obesity and cardiovascular disease, for children and adults (U.S. Department of Health & Human Services, 2008). Motor development and physical activity also seem to be intertwined. For example, improvements in motor development skills for children with ASD can support increases in physical activity by helping these children find ways to move more during the day.

When a child with ASD is taught how to throw and catch, then he or she is more likely to try out these skills during recess, on the playground, or in gym class. In a sense, this is a means to an end. Most types of physical activity require a threshold level of motor development skills. Therefore, children need to have good balance skills as they run around on the playground equipment, and need to be able to catch or throw to play games with balls. In addition, there is a social component to these types of physical activities that will be discussed in more depth later.

Researchers have found multiple benefits to increasing opportunities for physical activity, including effects related to classroom engagement, behavior, and academic performance (see, e.g., Howie, Beets, & Pate, 2014). They have also found that simultaneously focusing on physical activity and complex motor movements has multiple benefits on the brain and ultimately on observable behaviors, such as learning, attention, and mood improvements. These connections will be highlighted throughout this chapter.

In this book, physical activity is defined as "any body movement that works your muscles and requires more energy than resting" (U.S. Department of Health & Human Services, 2011, p. 1). Exercise will be defined as "a form of physical activity that is planned, structured, repetitive and performed with the goal of improving health or fitness" (U.S. Department of Health & Human Services, 2011, p. 7). Therefore, any movement that is encouraged during an intervention program to support motor development and increase activity will be defined as physical activity. Some of the activities will also be defined as exercise, and will typically have a target range for heart rate to make the activity strenuous.

National guidelines on physical activity suggest preschool-age children engage in at least 120 minutes of accumulated physical activity each day, with 60 minutes in structured activities and 60 minutes in unstructured activities (National Association for Sport and Physical Education, 2009). Guidelines for children older than six include at least 60 minutes per day of activity, and the majority of that activity should be aerobic (U.S. Department of Health & Human Services, 2008). In the end, the goal is to have children engage more frequently in exercise, since the benefits are clear.

Teachers have consistently reported positive changes in classroom performance in an area typically referred to as "readiness skills." Readiness skills include such activities as waiting for a turn, following directions, imitation, attention, and participation. On-task behavior increased for 4th and 5th graders after only 10 minutes of exercise (Howie et al., 2014). The biggest connection seems to be that exercise increases attention to tasks, thereby increasing engagement and learning.

Some studies also note that exercise may not only increase attention, but also increase the ability of the brain to process and store newly acquired knowledge or skills (see, e.g., Winter et al. 2007). Winter and colleagues found that typically developing adults learned vocabulary words more quickly following intense exercise (sprints) than after moderate running or sedentary exercise.

Although most studies examining the effects of exercise on the brain have studied animals and adults, the results have been noteworthy. Research has noted that increasing physical activity can have positive effects related to cardiovascular health, musculoskeletal health, obesity (Strong et al., 2005), learning, reductions in symptoms of obsessive-compulsive disorder (OCD), and reductions in stress, anxiety, and depression.

Prevalence rates for obesity are rising for adults and children, and may be higher for individuals with ASD. The prevalence rate for children with ASD are 30 percent, compared to a rate of 24 percent for age-matched peers (Curtin, Anderson, Must, & Bandini, 2010). Children with ASD may have even higher rates of obesity than children with other developmental disabilities, such as learning disabilities or ADHD (Chen, Kim, Houtrow, & Newacheck, 2009).

Obesity is related to long-term health concerns, such as diabetes, increased cardiovascular risk, stigma, and depression (Srinivasan, Pescatello, & Bhat, 2014). We know that children gain weight when they consume more calories than they burn during the day. Therefore, effective support should involve increasing physical activity during the day in order to use more calories.

Children with ASD are less active than their peers during the day (Pan, 2011). A number of factors may contribute to lower levels of activity, such as children avoiding activities or play that provide intensive sensory input, motor development delays, restricted interests, adherence to inflexible schedules, or a preference for predictable and structured activities, but targeted support can make an impact. These are all important areas to consider when planning or implementing a physical activity program.

Children who are active tend to stay active, and those who are not tend to remain less active than their peers, even into adulthood (Pate, Baranowski, Dowda, & Trost, 1996). One key to increasing physical activity levels is to help children learn fundamental movement skills that include activities such as kicking, throwing, balancing, running, and hopping (Alhassan et al., 2012).

Chapters 4 and 5 will discuss how teachers can focus on motor development in a systematic way during a physical activity program. For example, early in the program, activities will focus on skills such as balance and tracking (like tracking a balloon as it falls). These skills are imbedded into most sports, games, and activities with peers. Later, activities will progress to skills such as throwing, kicking, and catching.

Research has identified a number of mechanisms that may be creating changes in the brain when we engage in physical activity. The system is very complex, but a few key areas seem to be connected to physical activity and complex motor movements. Two significant chemical classes in the brain are involved (such as brain-derived neurotrophic factor [BDNF]) and neurotransmitters (such as serotonin, norepinephrine, and dopamine).

John Ratey, in his book *Spark* (2008), discusses these processes. He refers to BDNF as "Miracle-Gro for the brain" (p. 42), because it seems to be related to a number of processes that build, strengthen, and maintain connections in the brain. Exercise seems to significantly increase levels of BDNF in our brains. Ratey (2008) uses an analogy to compare neurons to trees: neurons have dendrites instead of branches, and synapses instead of leaves.

BDNF improves most functions of the neurons, including supporting growth of new dendrites, improving the signal strength between synapses, and protecting against decay. Therefore, as we learn new material, the presence of BDNF helps to build and strengthen these connections. Neeper and colleagues (1996) were the first to see this when they tested BDNF levels in mice during voluntary running. The more nights the mice ran, the more BDNF was present in their brains.

In another study, Klintsova and colleagues (2004) compared running rats to rats performing complex motor skills, such as walking across balance beams and rope ladders. After two weeks, the rats performing complex motor movements had a 35 percent increase in BDNF in their cerebellums, but the rats that just ran had none in that area. This provides evidence that a program should include both aerobic exercise and skill acquisition, or complex motor movements that require individuals to think about their movements, in order to maximize the benefits that children will receive.

The other compounds of note are neurotransmitters such as serotonin, norepinephrine, and dopamine. Exercise also seems to increase their levels in our brain. Serotonin is related to brain activity and influences areas such as mood, impulsivity, anger, and aggression. The drug Prozac affects serotonin levels, and has been used to treat depression, anxiety, and obsessive compulsive disorder (OCD). Norepinephrine is associated with attention, perception, motivation, and arousal.

Finally, dopamine is associated with learning, satisfaction, attention, and movement. Increasing and moderating levels of these compounds in the brain through physical activity can lead to multiple benefits for children with ASD. It is a natural way to regulate brain activity.

THE CHALLENGE FOR CHILDREN WITH ASD

For most children, motor skills develop naturally during activities such as running, jumping, and throwing or catching a ball. However, some young children, especially children with ASD, fail to develop proficient motor skills and, consequently, are less likely to engage in these activities. They may even experience negative health outcomes across their lifespan, including obesity (Srinivasan et al., 2014), cardiovascular disease, high blood pressure, and poor self-concept (Sutherland, Couch, & Iacono, 2002).

Although motor-skill deficits are not listed as a specific diagnostic characteristic used to identify ASD (APA, 2013), young children with ASD often experience significant delays in motor development, such as delays in overall gross motor skills, manual dexterity, balance, gait, motor coordination, and ball-handling skills (Fournier, Hass, Naik, Lodha, & Cauraugh, 2010). Pan (2011) also notes that children with ASD are less active than their typically developing peers, and have been found to engage in physical activity for less than half of recess or free play times. It is important to find ways to get children with ASD more active during the day.

In fact, recent research indicates that two- to three-year-old children with ASD may even experience regression in motor skills, and that could continue into preschool and elementary school (Bhat, Landa, & Galloway, 2011; Lloyd, MacDonald, & Lord, 2011). One theory is that children are losing motor skills due to limited physical activity and opportunities to practice motor movements.

As children get older, many motor skills are intertwined with social interactions. For example, they may be running around or climbing on playground equipment with peers during recess or free time after school. Or they are kicking and throwing balls during organized sports or games at school. These practice opportunities are combined with peer interactions. Children need to know how to perform the skills. They also need to want to enter the activity, and know how to navigate the social interactions that are part of the game.

It appears that a cycle is created in which children with ASD tend to stay by themselves on the edges of the playground for two main reasons: motor and social. First, motor delays make it difficult to perform skills required on the playground or sports field. Second, social delays make it more difficult for them to navigate entering the game and maneuvering the rules once they do. Therefore, there are challenges in both the motor domain and the social domain. Below I address motor skills; social skills will be examined in more depth in the next chapter.

BENEFITS OF INCREASED MOTOR DEVELOPMENT AND PHYSICAL ACTIVITY

Research has demonstrated that learning is impacted by physical activity in multiple areas, including executive functioning, cognition, and memory. For example, Kramer and colleagues (1999) examined the effects of exercise on executive functioning skills (e.g., planning, scheduling, inhibition, working memory) for previously sedentary adults. Treatment compared aerobic walking with anaerobic stretching.

Most notably, improvements were noted for the walking group in tests involving planning, scheduling, inhibition, and working memory. They also noted gains on a test that measures one's ability to adapt to new situations. This is a particular concern for individuals with ASD, and an impact here would be significant.

Winter and colleagues (2007) also noted that people learned vocabulary words 20 percent faster after exercise than before it. This finding suggests that learning rate increases through exercise as the levels of BDNF increase. Other research has noted that the intensity of physical activity is associated with cognitive performance, processing speed, memory, and mental flexibility (Angevarena et al., 2007). Improvements have been noted after just the first exercise session.

In a literature review, Ploughman (2008) found that exercise increased brain volume in areas that affect executive functioning, improved cognition in children with cerebral palsy, and improved phonemic skills in children with reading difficulties. Although the optimal time for learning appears to be immediately following exercise, levels of all compounds in the brain will increase over time and lead to long-term change.

Anxiety affects about 18 percent of the overall population, and seems to be a concern for many children with ASD. Exercise has shown positive effects in reducing stress and anxiety. Increased levels of BDNF after exercise may help strengthen new brain connections and reduce anxiety. Broocks and colleagues (1998) compared exercise to drug therapy for panic disorder for 10 weeks. The treatment groups included: (a) regular exercise, (b) a daily dose of clomipramine, and (c) a daily placebo pill. Both the exercise group and the clomipramine group were at the same level after 10 weeks of treatment.

More recently, Broman-Fulks and colleagues (2004) examined exercise as a treatment for anxiety sensitivity. Treatment included either running on a treadmill at 60 percent to 90 percent of maximum heart rate, or walking at approximately 50 percent of maximum heart rate. Strenuous exercise worked more quickly and effectively. Exercise also seems to reduce levels of stress that can be related to anxiety.

Lastly, there has been significant research on the effects of exercise on depression. About 17 percent of American adults experience depression at some point. Individuals with ASD may also experience depression symptoms. Though reported prevalence rates vary, they seem to be at least as high as those seen in the general population (Stewart, Barnard, Pearson, Hasan, & O'Brien, 2006). The highest reported rate was 34 percent.

Depression may be difficult to detect in children with ASD due to communication deficits, and rates may increase for older children (Stewart et al., 2006). Ratey (2008) states that "exercise counters depression at almost every level" (p. 114). In fact, effective treatments for depression include norepinephrine, dopamine, and serotonin, which are all elevated during exercise.

Blumenthal and colleagues (1999) conducted a major study on depression that compared the effects of exercise and those of Zoloft. The groups included (a) Zoloft, (b) exercise, and (c) both. The exercise group engaged in supervised walking or jogging at 70–85 percent maximum heart rate for 30 minutes (including a 10-minute warm up and 5-minute cool down), three times per week. All three groups had a significant drop in depression, and about half of each group were considered to be in remission. The authors concluded that exercise was as effective as drug treatment.

Overall, exercise seemed to take longer to produce effects, but may be better over the long term since it provided participants with a level of control over their own symptoms without the side effects of medication. Strenuous exercise also produces endorphins that help calm the brain, relieve pain, and help people feel good. These could all be positive for children with ASD.

Recently, research has begun to track the effects of exercise on individuals with ASD. Results relate to earlier findings in animal and adult studies. Lang and colleagues (2010) conducted one major review that examined the effects of exercise on individuals with ASD, based upon 18 studies. All studies reported improvements in behavior, academics, physical fitness, or increased exercise behaviors. Specifically, the authors noted improvements in behavior that included reduced stereotypy (or repeated movement like pacing or hand flapping), aggression, self-injury, and disruptive behaviors. Although stereotypy was not a commonly reported change, reductions through physical activity would be significant for practitioners, families, and individuals with ASD.

Lang and colleagues hypothesized that exercise may provide input that is similar to the function of the stereotypy, and therefore reduces the need to engage in the unexpected behavior. It may also be possible to match the activity in an intervention with the child's stereotypy, such as hand flapping or pacing, by having children throw or practice the throwing motion and run laps or back and forth in a classroom or hallway.

Improvements in academics included increases in time on task, accuracy in responding, vocabulary, and responses to demands or questions. Improvements in physical fitness included increased endurance or strength, flexibility, and aerobic fitness. Lang and colleagues also noted that participants spent more time engaged in exercise.

OPTIMIZING THE EFFECTS OF PHYSICAL ACTIVITY AND EXERCISE

Overall, the available research and guidelines suggest that there are positive outcomes from increasing physical activity and complex motor movements for children with ASD. Important components to include in a physical activity program are discussed in chapters 4 and 5. The intervention should last for about 30 minutes, and include:

- 10 minutes of exercise that results in an increased heart rate
- 10–15 minutes of motor development that should naturally include complex motor movements (such as balancing, throwing, catching)

- 5-minute cool down (such as meditation or yoga) that can help the kids get calm again and ready to learn

TAKEAWAYS

1. Practitioners should combine motor development and exercise. Something about this combination increases levels of BDNF in the brain and improves outcomes associated with engaging in either exercise or complex motor movements in isolation.
2. Get children moving for at least 10 minutes. Having kids engage in exercise for just 10 minutes seems to improve their ability to pay attention to what is happening in the classroom.
3. The benefits of increased BDNF, such as strengthening neuronal connections in the brain, seem to improve memory and rate of learning.
4. The benefits of increased neurotransmitters, such as serotonin and dopamine, seem to include improved attention and motivation, and reduced impulsivity and aggression.

REFERENCES

Alhassan, S., Nwaokelemeh, O., Ghazarian, M., Roberts, J., Mendoza, A., & Shitole, S. (2012). Effects of locomotor skill program on minority preschoolers' physical activity levels. *Pediatric Exercise Science, 24*, 435–49.

American Psychiatric Association (APA). (2013). *Diagnostic and statistical manual of mental disorders* (5th ed.). Arlington, VA: Author.

Angevarena, M., Vanhees'a, L., Wendel-Vosc, W., Verhaarb, H. J. J., Aufdemkampea, G., Alemand, A., & Verschurenc, W. M. M. (2007). Intensity, but not duration, of physical activities is related to cognitive function. *Cardiac & Cardiovascular Systems, 14*(6), 825–30.

Bhat, A. N., Landa, R. J., & Galloway, J. C. (2011). Current perspectives on motor functioning in infants, children, and adults with autism spectrum disorders. *Physical Therapy, 91*(7), 1116–29.

Blumenthal, J. A., Babyak, M. A., Moore, K. A., Craighead, W. E., Herman, S., Khatri, P., Waugh, R., Napolitano, M. A., et al. (1999). Effects of exercise training on older patients with major depression. *Archives of Internal Medicine, 159*, 2349–56.

CHAPTER 2

Broman-Fulks, J., Berman, M. E., Rabian, B. A., & Webster, M. J. (2004). Effects of aerobic exercise on anxiety sensitivity. *Behavior Research & Therapy, 42*, 125–36.

Broocks, A., Bandelow, B., Pekrun, G., George, A., Meyer, T., Bartmann, U., Hillmer-Vogel, U., & Rüther, E. (1998). Comparison of aerobic exercise, clomipramine, and placebo in the treatment of panic disorder. *The American Journal of Psychiatry, 155*(5), 603–9.

Chen, A. Y., Kim, S. E., Houtrow, A. J., & Newacheck, P. W. (2009). Prevalence of obesity among children with chronic conditions. *Obesity, 18*, 210–13.

Curtin, C., Anderson, S. E., Must, A., & Bandini, L. (2010). The prevalence of obesity in children with autism: A secondary data analysis using nationally representative data from the National Survey of Children's Health. *BMC Pediatrics, 10*, 11.

Fournier, K. A., Hass, C. J., Naik, S. K., Lodha, N., & Cauraugh, J. H. (2010). Motor coordination in autism spectrum disorders: A synthesis and meta-analysis. *Journal of Autism and Developmental Disorders, 40,* 1227–40. doi:10.1007/s10803-010-0981-3

Howie, E. K., Beets, M. W., & Pate, R. R. (2014). Acute classroom exercise breaks improved on-task behavior in 4th and 5th grade students: A dose response. *Mental Health and Physical Activity, 7,* 65–71.

Klintsova, A. Y., Dickson, E., Yoshida, R., & Greenough, W. T. (2004). Altered expression of BDNF and its high-affinity receptor TrkB in response to complex motor learning and moderate exercise. *Brain Research, 1028,* 92–104.

Kramer, A. F., Hahn, S., Cohen, N. J., Banich, M. T., McAuley, E., Harrison, C. R., et al. (1999). Aging, fitness, and neurocognitive functioning. *Nature, 400,* 418–19.

Lang, R., Koegel, L. K., Ashbaugh, K., Regester, A., Ence, W., & Smith, W. (2010). Physical exercise and individuals with autism spectrum disorders: A systematic review. *Research in Autism Spectrum Disorders, 4*, 565–76.

Lloyd, M., MacDonald, M., & Lord, C. (2011). Motor skills of toddlers with autism spectrum disorders. *Autism, 17*, 133–46. doi:10.1177/1362361311402230

National Association for Sport and Physical Education. (2009). *Active Start* (2nd ed.). Oxon Hill: AAHPERD Publications.

Neeper, S. A., Gómez-Pinilla, F., Choi, J., & Cotman, C. W. (1996). Physical activity increases mRNA for brain-derived neurotrophic factor and nerve growth factor in rat brain. *Brain Research, 726* (1–2), 49–56.

Pan, C. Y. (2011). The efficacy of an aquatic program on physical fitness and aquatic skills in children with and without autism spectrum disorders. *Research in Autism Spectrum Disorders, 5*, 657–65.

Pate, R. R., Baranowski, T., Dowda, M., & Trost, S. G. (1996). Tracking of physical activity in young children. *Medicine & Science in Sports & Exercise, 28*(1), 92–96.

Ploughman, M. (2008). Exercise is brain food: The effects of physical activity on cognitive functioning. *Developmental Neurorehabilitation, 11*(3), 236–40.

Ratey, J. J., with Hagerman, E. (2008). *Spark: The revolutionary new science of exercise and the brain.* New York: Little, Brown & Company.

Srinivasan, S. M., Pescatello, L. S., & Bhat, A. N. (2014). Current perspectives on physical activity and exercise recommendations for children and adolescents with autism spectrum disorders. *Physical Therapy, 94*(6), 875–89.

Stewart, M. E., Barnard, L., Pearson, J., Hasan, R., & O'Brien, G. (2006). Presentation of depression in autism and Asperger syndrome: A review. *Autism, 10*(1), 103–16. doi:10.1177/1362361306062013

Strong, W. B., Malina, R. M., Blimkie, C. J., Daniels, S. R., Dishman, R. K., Gutin, B., & Trudeau, F. (2005). Evidence based physical activity for school-age youth. *Journal of Pediatrics, 146,* 732–37. doi:10.1016/j.jpeds.2005.01.055

Sutherland, G., Couch, M. A., & Iacono, T. (2002). Health issues for adults with developmental disability. *Research in Developmental Disabilities, 23*(6), 422–45. doi:10.1016/S0891-4222(02)00143-9

U.S. Department of Health & Human Services. (2008). *Physical activity guidelines for Americans.* Washington, DC: Author.

U.S. Department of Health & Human Services. (2011). *What is physical activity?* Washington, DC: Author. http://www.nhlbi.nih.gov/health/health-topics/topics/phys

Winter, B., Breitenstein, C., Mooren, F. C., Voelker, K., Fobker, M., Lechtermann, A., Krueger, K., Fromme, A., Korsukewitz, C., Floel, A., & Knecht, S. (2007). High impact running improves learning. *Neurobiology of Learning and Memory, 87,* 597–609.

3

CONNECTIONS BETWEEN MOTOR AND SOCIAL DEVELOPMENT

LINKS BETWEEN MOTOR AND SOCIAL DEVELOPMENT

Two key areas impact social development for children with ASD. First, negative social and academic outcomes from preschool into adulthood have been linked to deficits in children's social behaviors (e.g., Bramlett, Scott, & Rowell, 2000; Gest, Sesma, Masten, & Tellegen, 2006). Second, children with ASD experience increased social stress as they get older, therefore it is crucial that educators in pre-K and elementary school settings focus on social skills for children with ASD (Rotherham-Fuller, Kasari, Chamberlain, & Locke, 2010).

Without targeted intervention support, it is likely that problems with social interactions will persist and may even worsen as children progress though elementary school (Rotherham-Fuller et al., 2010). Physical activity programs are an ideal time to support social skill development. This chapter will focus upon key links between motor and social development, and presents a framework that will be used in future chapters to provide focused support during motor activity programs.

Bhat and colleagues (2011) propose that a developmental link exists between motor and social communication impairments in autism that makes movement fundamental to social interaction. Recent research has highlighted multiple links between movement and social skills, especially during the period of early childhood. These include connections with brain development, communication, motor skills, and free time activities such as active play.

Brain-derived neurotrophic factor (BDNF) and the neurotransmitters serotonin, epinephrine, and dopamine seem to play a key role in the connection between movement and social skill development. As discussed in chapter 2, exercise increases levels of all these compounds in the brain, and each has an effect on the social domain. For example, serotonin affects mood, impulsivity, and self-esteem, and reduces stress, depression, and OCD symptoms. Each of these changes has social implications. For example, if we feel better about ourselves, then we are more likely to interact with others.

Similarly, dopamine improves mood, and increases attention and motivation. Attention and focus allow us to attend to important information in the environment, such as peer interactions, and improve our ability to respond positively to direct instruction in social skills. Norepinephrine activates the brain to support learning new skills and improving self-esteem. Finally, BDNF levels rise in the brain during exercise, and this supports improved function on all levels within our neurons. Therefore, new material is more quickly learned and retained.

Research also suggests that there are crucial links between movement and other areas of development, such as communication (Iverson, 2010; Seymour, Reid, & Bloom, 2009). For example, children's motor development during the first 18 months of life provides opportunities for expanding communicative development (including nonverbal communication) and language acquisition, and children who have significant motor delays may miss these opportunities (Iverson, 2010). Even small deficits in early emerging developmental skills can have far-reaching effects on other areas of development, such as oral language production and nonverbal communication skills (Iverson, 2010).

Another area of focus for children with ASD has been theory of mind (ToM). ToM refers to an individual's ability to understand what other people are thinking, or the ability to take another person's perspective (Baron-Cohen, 1989; Premack & Woodruff, 1978). Essentially it means that we can understand that another person's beliefs can differ from our own. ToM and pretend play seem to be connected through early skills that both concepts share: (a) social referencing, (b) joint attention, and (c) reading intentions.

Social referencing typically develops by the time a child is 12 months old, and involves the ability to pick up on cues from an adult or play partner about an event. Parents may provide these cues to children through facial expressions, mistimed gestures, and/or looking more frequently at the child. Similarly, 12-month-old children are typically able to engage in joint attention. This includes the ability to point to an object or event to share something with an adult, or to follow the adult pointing out an object of interest. Motor delays, however, can impact joint attention (initiating, responding to others) by affecting young children's abilities to turn their head, reach, point, and give and show objects (Gernsbacher, Stevenson, Khandaker, & Goldsmith, 2008). Finally, by 30 months, children are typically able to understand the intentions of others.

Movement is intricately tied to social development through play. There are a few key things to consider as play develops for children during the preschool and elementary school years. The most common features of play include:

- Pleasure
- Active engagement
- Personally motivated
- Use of familiar objects or exploration of unfamiliar objects (Fromberg, 1998; Rubin, Fein, & Vandenberg, 1983).

These features can also be easily incorporated within a physical activity program, and the skills learned during the program can transfer to play opportunities with peers. Play becomes more complex over time, and is interwoven with motor and social skills. For example, children need a play partner to practice skills such as balance, jumping, and running when they play chase or tag during recess.

One idea to consider is how children move during play episodes. This is referred to as locomotion. Locomotion involves moving from one place to another and includes crawling, walking, running, hopping, and jumping forward. Research has connected locomotion with communication through gestural communication and object sharing. Deficits in locomotion may translate to deficits in these areas as well (Karasik, Tamis-LeMonda, & Adolph, 2011).

Play is also physical. Piaget (1962) proposed three main stages of play development: (a) exercise play (functional), (b) symbolic play, and (c) games with rules. In the first stage, children from birth to two years engage in functional play for the pleasure of the activity (e.g., shaking a rattle). Many young children with ASD may still need support to develop functional play skills that involve motor movements. Many of these are connected to social skills due to their reliance on a peer connection for practice (Lloyd et al., 2011).

Children also need the skills to play appropriately. In the final stage, children from seven to eleven years old engage in games with rules (e.g., hopscotch, marbles) that are passed from child to child (Piaget & Inhelder, 1969). These games create opportunities for children to practice taking turns, following rules, and engaging in social interactions. In order for children to be able to engage with peers in games that have rules, for example, they must engage in such skills as entering group play, initiating and responding to interactions, and resolving conflicts. The stages of play progressively build on each other and require increasingly higher levels of cognition, language, and social skills.

Vygotsky (1967) also developed his own series of play stages. First, children need the *motor* skills to engage in athletic games. Second, they also need *social* skills such as flexibility, entering, initiating/responding to peers, and resolving conflicts. Third, rules become more focused over time, and are necessary for children to retain interest as they get older.

Play for preschoolers may conform to certain rules of behavior, as mentioned earlier, but it is more flexible than the play of older children, and may change from moment to moment (Vygotsky, 1967). We can see that children's play becomes more complex over time as they build on previously learned skills and are able to explore the boundaries between real and imaginary as their pretend-play skills develop.

Pellegrini (1992) observed children during recess and compared the amount of time children engaged with peers in cooperative behavior (e.g., games, conversation), and in adult-directed behavior. Children who interacted more frequently with peers during recess in kindergarten had higher academic achievement in first grade. In fact, recess behaviors were a stronger predictor of first grade academic achievement than kindergarten achievement.

Pellegrini's findings also indicated that peer interaction was positively related to achievement, while adult-directed behavior was negatively related to achievement. Children who preferred to play with peers performed better than those who interacted more with adults. It is often easier for children to interact with adults, because adults make allowances for unusual behaviors, work with children to repair communication breakdowns, and will play with the child's chosen activities. Typically developing peers may not make these allowances.

Recess is an important time for learning, yet teachers often fail to have time to support it during a busy school day. By creating opportunities for motor development and focusing on social interaction skills during a physical activity program, children are more likely to be appropriately engaged on the playground.

Social skills can also be impacted by delays in motor development. One way this occurs may be due to limited opportunities to engage in active play (see, e.g., Pellegrini & Smith, 1998). Active play or exercise play is defined as using gross motor movements during play (Pellegrini & Smith, 1998). Active play appears to peak during the preschool years when children are four to five years old (Eaton & Yu, 1989).

Research suggests that active play supports strength development, skill development, increased endurance (Byers & Walker, 1995), and may promote the development of social skills, daily living skills, and adaptive behavior (Lloyd et al., 2011).

Since play is difficult for children with ASD due to motor, communication, and social deficits, they may miss crucial opportunities to practice and learn new gross motor skills. According to Lloyd and colleagues (2011), this creates a scenario in which "poor motor skills constrain social interactions and poor social interactions constrain motor skill development" (p. 14). Therefore, according to Srinivasan and colleagues (2014), "Addressing motor deficiencies and physical activity levels may indirectly affect the core social communication impairments of individuals with ASDs by providing greater opportunities for socialization with peers, better attentional focus, and improved motor performance" (p. 883).

Ways in which classroom teachers can embed social interactions into a physical activity program are outlined in chapter 6. For example, most of the opportunities to practice motor skills will include a social component, since this is how these skills are practiced in real life. Children can work with partners to throw or kick balls, and engage in activities like obstacle courses.

Teachers can embed any motor activity into an obstacle course (e.g., balance, jumping, throwing), and a course can be used to practice social skills (e.g., taking turns and waiting). Children also watch their peers complete the activities, cheer their peers on, and smile or laugh as they work through the obstacle course. These activities also all link to the playground, recess area, or home where children can use their new skills. Kids have become more engaged on the playground, even creating their own obstacle course, and parents have described the new games they have played at home.

IMPLICATIONS FOR CLASSROOM PERFORMANCE AND SUPPORT

There are several ideas to consider when supporting social development in the classroom during a physical activity program. For example, teachers and practitioners should keep the motor programs fun, with a play-based component. Children will develop confidence through success in these programs, and that tends to translate to other areas. Children with ASD should be more engaged outside on the playground, during free time in the classroom, and during activities at home or in the community.

The key is to create opportunities for social success during and outside of the motor program. This includes a combination of strategies that are categorized based on McConnell's (2002) classifications. These include

- Environmental modifications (such as using a predictable routine, selecting preferred activities, and including the home and other settings).
- Child-specific support (such as direct instruction in initiations and responses).
- Collateral skills support (such as using preferred games or activities, teaching the necessary skills to engage with the game or activity, and matching skills to the developmental level).
- Peer-mediated support (such as training peers to work with targeted children, or self-selecting peers to be in groups with or near targeted children).

These strategies will be discussed in more detail in chapter 6.

TAKEAWAYS

1. Since motor and social skills are connected, teachers should ensure that opportunities for social interaction are embedded into physical activity programs. These social interactions can include taking turns, using joint attention, and following directions.
2. Social development is as important as academic development for children with ASD. Physical activity programs are another way to practice these skills and to create positive peer experiences.
3. Activities like obstacle courses are a great way to practice skills, especially social skills. For example, teachers can turn the obstacle course into a relay race, and students can practice skills such as waiting, taking turns, an attending to their peers (and cheering) as they complete the course.

REFERENCES

Baron-Cohen, S. (1989). The autistic child's theory of mind: A case of specific developmental delay. *Journal of Child Psychology and Psychiatry, 30*(2), 285–97.

Bhat, A. N., Landa, R. J., & Galloway, J. C. (2011). Current perspectives on motor functioning in infants, children, and adults with autism spectrum disorders. *Physical Therapy, 91*(7), 1116–29.

Bramlett, R. K., Scott, P., & Rowell, R. K. (2000). A comparison of temperament and social skills in predicting academic performance in first grade. *Special Services in the Schools, 16*(1), 147–58.

Byers, J. A., & Walker, C. (1995). Refining the motor training hypothesis for the evolution of play. *American Naturalist, 146,* 25–40.

Eaton, W. C., & Yu, A. P. (1989). Are sex differences in child motor activity level a function of sex differences in maturational level? *Child Development, 60,* 1005–11.

Fromberg, D. P. (1998). Play issues in early childhood education. In C. Seefeldt & A. Galper (Eds.), *Continuing issues in early childhood education* (2nd ed.) (pp. 190–206). Upper Saddle River, NJ: Prentice Hall.

Gernsbacher, M. A., Stevenson, J. L., Khandaker, S., & Goldsmith, H. H. (2008). Why does joint attention look atypical in autism? *Child Development Perspectives, 2,* 38–45.

Gest, S. D., Sesma, A., Jr., Masten, A. S., & Tellegen, A. (2006). Childhood peer reputation as a predictor of competence and symptoms 10 years later. *Journal of Abnormal Child Psychology, 34*(4), 509–26.

Iverson, J. M. (2010). Developing language in a developing body: The relationship between motor development and language development. *Journal of Child Language, 37*, 229–61.

Karasik, L. B., Tamis-LeMonda, C. S., & Adolph, K. E. (2011). Transition from crawling to walking and infants' actions with objects and people. *Child Development, 82*(4), 1199–1209.

Lloyd, M., MacDonald, M., & Lord, C. (2011). Motor skills of toddlers with autism spectrum disorders. *Autism, 17*, 133–46. doi:10.1177/1362361311402230

McConnell, S. R. (2002). Interventions to facilitate social interaction for young children with autism: Review of available research and recommendations for educational intervention and future research. *Journal of Autism and Developmental Disorders, 32*(5), 351–72.

Pellegrini, A. D. (1992). Kindergarten children's social cognitive status as a predictor of first grade success. *Early Childhood Research Quarterly*, 7(4), 565–77.

Pellegrini, A. D., & Smith, P. K. (1998). Physical activity play: The nature and function of a neglected aspect of play. *Child Development, 69*(3), 577–98.

Piaget, J. (1962). *Play, dreams and imitation in childhood.* New York: W. W. Norton & Company, Inc.

Piaget, J., & Inhelder, B. (1969). *The psychology of the child.* New York: Basic Books, Inc.

Premack, D., & Woodruff, G. (1978). Does the chimpanzee have a theory of mind? *Behavioral and Brain Sciences, 1*, 515–26.

Rotherham-Fuller, E., Kasari, C., Chamberlain, B., & Locke, J. (2010). Social involvement of children with autism spectrum disorders in elementary classrooms. *Journal of Child Psychology and Psychiatry, 51(11)*, 1227–34.

Rubin, K. H., Fein, G. G., & Vandenberg, B. (1983). Play. In E. M. Hetherington (Ed.), P. H. Mussen (Series Ed.), *Handbook of Child Psychology: Vol. 4. Socialization, personality, and social development* (pp. 693–741). New York: Wiley.

Seymour, H., Reid, G., & Bloom, G. A. (2009). Friendship in inclusive physical education. *Adapted Physical Education Quarterly, 26*, 201–19.

Srinivasan, S. M., Pescatello, L. S., & Bhat, A. N. (2014). Current perspectives on physical activity and exercise recommendations for children and adolescents with autism spectrum disorders. *Physical Therapy, 94*(6), 875–89.

Vygotsky, L. S. (1967). Play and its role in the mental development of the child. *Soviet Psychology, 5*(3), 6–18.

4

SETTING UP THE ENVIRONMENT

KEY IDEAS FOR ORGANIZATION

It's important for any intervention implemented in the classroom, including a physical activity program, to proactively address potential areas of concern for kids with ASD. These ideas were introduced in chapter 1 and will be discussed further in this chapter to offer information about structure, setting, materials, frequency and duration, teacher/child ratios, and the developmental progressions of skills.

Structure

The structure that works best may depend on the children in your class and the activities you choose. In general, both the activity/exercise and cool down/meditation segments of the program will run well as a whole-group activity, with adults available for support. It may work well to break the class into groups for the motor development segment. This will allow for more individualized attention and frequent opportunities for children to practice skills.

Group structure is important. Teachers should consider the benefits of creating groups that have mixed abilities or groups where all the children have similar abilities. If the groups have mixed abilities, then more proficient peers can serve as models and peer partners. If the groups have similar abilities, then teachers can match the pace of the groups with their skill levels. In this model, some groups will move slower and some groups will move faster. Teachers can match the focus skills of the activity with the needs of group members, or set up stations and have groups rotate through the activities.

For example, if the groups are matched by ability and the target skill is learning to throw one-handed, then each group would be working on different skills. One group may be composed of children who can throw one-handed and have good technique. They may be working on distance and accuracy. The teacher could set up the activity so they throw back and forth with partners. The teacher could place tape on the floor or use floor markers to create different distances. The other group may still be working on proper form and accuracy from a short distance. Again, they could be paired with partners. The teacher may also use floor markers to demonstrate correct foot placement during the throw. Since this group needs additional help, the teacher may work with this group or have extra support in this group to practice with each child or pair as they throw.

Another consideration for teachers is how to limit or effectively use wait time. Wait time is interesting. In general, teachers should try to reduce it because the goal is to keep kids moving, and too much wait time can lead to behavioral problems. Since the ability to wait is an important skill, however, it may be one for teachers to encourage to some degree. Therefore, having some wait time for children can be positive. Many teachers have noticed that children's ability to wait for their turn improves as the program progresses. The key seems to be that teachers have a plan for what children will do while they wait, and that wait time is limited.

There are a few ways to address wait time. These include:

- Have a spot where each child waits, such as a chair or floor marker.
- Keep kids active while they wait. Add materials to play with such as scarves, balls, and beanbags, or have children perform extra activities while they wait, such as jumping jacks, running in place, or jumping and hopping in place.
- Encourage children to watch and cheer for their peers while they wait.

Activity choices will vary depending upon the size of the group. For example, you could have children who are working in a one-on-one situation, in small groups of two to eight children, or classrooms of fifteen to twenty-five students that include children with ASD. Each of these may look slightly different in their implementation.

- *One-on-one.* The teacher has complete flexibility with a one-on-one situation. You can develop a very structured program, but may want to let the child choose the activities at times. Develop a choice board, so the child has some level of control, but you are managing the options. For example, provide two or three options for activities that involve a target skill such as throwing. Then you know the child will practice the skill and will have added motivation, since he or she picked the activity.
- *Small group.* In a small-group situation the students would benefit from all engaging in the same activities. Embed some level of choice, and use activities you know the kids really like.
- *Large group.* In a large-group setting the teacher will want to run most of the activities as a whole group. If possible, you'll want to keep children with ASD engaged in the same activities as their peers. Just set the expectation that the child will complete the same activities as his or her peers. The teacher or any supporting adults can rotate around to provide support as needed. You can also pair children with a buddy to provide additional support during the activity. The exercise component and meditation/cool down can be run as a whole-group activity.

Setting

There are many ways to look at the setting of the program. In general, teachers should examine ways to use the available space and to recognize that a physical activity program can occur in multiple settings. For example, the activities could be implemented indoors or outdoors. If you stay indoors, then you could explore use of the classroom, hallways, gym, or other spaces in the school. If you stay outdoors, then you may want to look for a space that has fences or a clearly defined area, such as a blacktop or soccer field.

What space works for your students will depend on the children in your classroom. For example, if you have children in your class who are easily distracted, you would want to find a space that has fewer distractions, such as an empty classroom, or look for a time in the day when a space is quieter.

Teachers have used a variety of settings for physical activity programs, including classrooms, hallways, and common areas such as a gym or a multipurpose room. Selecting a space will depend both on your needs and space availability.

In one program, teachers began creating a schedule for a common room and even shared responsibility for setting up and cleaning up the space each day. This seemed to work well and saved time for everyone. Teachers could also start in their classroom and then use the hallway space for small groups or different activities, such as an obstacle course. These physical activity programs are flexible enough to be run in multiple spaces; kids generally can adapt to the space you use, or you can adapt the environment as needed. For example, materials can be transported each day, a schedule can be established for days or times during the week, or a space can be designated for the program.

Materials

There are a number of materials teachers can use when developing ideas for a physical activity program. The ones listed below are common ones that could be used across multiple activities. These can often be found at school, many teachers may already have these as part of existing supplies, or they can be purchased from various websites. One source is Flaghouse (www.flaghouse.com). Teachers should feel free to be creative about the materials they use, keeping safety and cost in mind. For example, the bricks or cones can be used with cones and bars to create multiple activities for both exercise and motor development programs. Bricks and bars can be set up to create jumps for children, or hoops can be placed on top of cones as targets for throwing balls or bean bags.

- Scarves
- Bubbles
- Balloons
- Floor markers (can be various colors or numbered)
- Balance beams (foam or 2 × 4 lumber)
- Different types of balls
    - Small (foam baseball, tennis ball, whiffle)
    - Large (kickball, beach ball, football, soccer ball, volley ball)
- Frisbee disks

- Bean bags
- Plastic paddles and bats
- Steeple bricks
- Large and small cones
- Long and short bars
- Large and small hoops
- Jump ropes
- Mats
- Twister game
- Volleyball nets
- Basketball nets
- Trampoline
- Scooters

Floor markers can be used in multiple ways during a physical activity program. For example, markers can help children understand where to stand or sit during activities or wait time. They can show children where to place their feet during activities like jumping or throwing. They can be used during obstacle courses or activities by having children practice motor movements such as sidestepping, hopping, or jumping on or between markers.

Floor markers can also be used to help children differentiate. For example, vary the distance between markers for children during jumping or throwing activities. Markers can also be numbered or color coordinated so children can practice counting or labeling colors as they move between markers. Lastly, numbered floor markers can help organize children's movements between activities. For example, use the #1 marker to designate the first activity, and then the #2 marker for the second activity. This will help create a structure and organize the activity session.

One teacher also used materials to practice important skills during cleanup time at the end of each session as another way to differentiate. For example, she would target specific skills such as differentiating objects ("Please pick up a floor marker"), colors ("Please pick up a red object"), and numbers ("Please pick up two objects"). Or she would target multistep directions by asking a child to "First, pick up the red hoop, and then pick up the blue marker," or saying, "Please pick up two red floor markers." The children really enjoyed the activity.

Frequency and Duration

Teachers should try to match the frequency and duration of a physical activity program with National Institutes of Health (NIH) guidelines to the greatest extent possible. These state that preschool children should engage in at least 120 minutes of accumulated physical activity each day, with at least 60 minutes in structured activities (National Association for Sport and Physical Education, 2009). Guidelines for children older than six include at least 60 minutes of physical activity per day, and the majority of that activity should be aerobic (U.S. Department of Health and Human Services, 2008).

Children will benefit from any amount of physical activity that can be added to the school day, but teachers may want to strive for 30 minutes, three times per week. This could also be achieved through a cumulative effect whereby teachers engage in activities for shorter amounts of time that add up to 20 minutes every day. For example, have the class or student engage in 10 minutes of exercise or motor development in between academic activities a twice a day. Or run a program that occurs every day for 20 minutes, and alternate between days that include exercise/cool down and days that include motor development/cool down. Table 4.1 includes three different ways to run a physical activity program: (a) every other day for 30 minutes, (b) every day for 20 minutes, and (c) twice per day.

Teachers may also be able to alternate between "exercise" and "complex motor movements" each day. In that case, you would keep the meditation as a cool down each time, and commit to 15–20 minutes every day. For example, Pangrazi and colleagues (2009) developed activity cards that involved exercise or activity breaks of 5–10 minutes throughout the day.

Child/Adult Ratio

The child-to-adult ratio depends on the needs of the children in your classroom and your comfort level with the activities. More adults can be helpful, but physical activity programs can be run successfully with one or two adults in both self-contained and inclusive environments. Having more support will help manage behaviors, and allow for individualized support as needed.

It may be possible to recruit families to come in to help, to have older children come to the classroom to work with your class, or to coordinate the physical activity program on certain days with an adaptive physical educa-

Table 4.1. Scheduling options for a physical activity program

A. Three days per week for both exercise and motor development

Monday	*Tuesday*	*Wednesday*	*Thursday*	*Friday*
30 minutes: physical activity program		30 minutes: physical activity program		30 minutes: physical activity program

B. Every day alternating exercise and motor development

Monday	*Tuesday*	*Wednesday*	*Thursday*	*Friday*
20 minutes: exercise & cool down	20 minutes: motor development & cool down	20 minutes: exercise & cool down	20 minutes: motor development & cool down	20 minutes: exercise & cool down

Note: Could alternate weeks so that one week includes three days of exercise and the next week includes three days of motor development.

C. Splitting exercise and motor development to include morning and afternoon sessions

Monday	*Tuesday*	*Wednesday*	*Thursday*	*Friday*
Morning: 10–15 minutes exercise & cool down		Morning: 10–15 minutes exercise & cool down		Morning: 10–15 minutes exercise & cool down
Afternoon: 10–15 minutes motor development & cool down		Afternoon: 10–15 minutes motor development & cool down		Afternoon: 10–15 minutes motor development & cool down

Note: Could also conduct motor development in the morning and exercise in the afternoon.

tion teacher, occupational therapist, or physical therapist in order to focus on the needs of specific children.

Developmental Progression

It is important that a physical activity program incorporates the teaching of new motor skills. These skills can follow a developmental progression and focus upon supporting children with delayed motor development. See table 4.2 for an outline of developmental milestones for children from three to nine years old.

Table 4.2. Gross motor skills by age

Age	*Developmental Milestones*
Three years	• Runs smoothly • Climbs stairs by alternating feet • Throws balls overhand; frequently catches a ball with arms fully extended; able to throw toward a target three feet away • Jumps off one step • Jumps in place • Pedals a tricycle • Pumps a swing
Four years	• Shows improved balance • Hops on one foot without losing balance • Throws a ball overhand with coordination; able to throw a ball forward five to seven feet toward a target • Walks heel-to-toe • Skips clumsily (skipping is a difficult gross motor pattern because it requires sequencing of a rhythmic pattern—a step and a hop) • Runs easily • Walks downstairs by alternating feet • Balances on one foot for five or more seconds • Catches a ball thrown at five feet • Steers and maneuvers a tricycle • Throws with forward weight shifting
Five years	• Develops increased coordination • Skips, jumps, and hops with good balance • Maintains balance while standing on one foot for several seconds • Skips with coordination • Walks backward with heel-toe pattern • Uses hands more than arms to catch a ball • Jumps down three or four steps • Jumps rope • Able to throw at a target overhand and underhand at a distance of five feet; refinement is seen over the next few years as distance and accuracy improve
Six to nine years	• Hops, skips, jumps; throws, catches, and kicks a ball (by age six) ◦ Accuracy, distance, and endurance increase with age ◦ Refinement in throwing continues as distance and accuracy improve; able to hit a target 12 feet away with overhand throw ◦ Runs and changes directions with increased accuracy ◦ Balance and coordination improve • This allows for proficiency in sports and agility in dance. Previously acquired skills are refined. Skills improve due to increases in muscle coordination and reaction time. • School-age children usually have smooth and strong motor skills. However, their coordination (especially eye-hand), endurance, balance, and physical abilities vary. • Motor play at this stage involves common components including: turn-taking, organization, role assignments, and rough-and-tumble play. Improvements in motor skills, along with cognitive and social development, help children to engage in games with rules.

Sources: Adapted from Case-Smith, J., & O'Brien, J. C. (2010); National Institutes of Health (2011); University of New Hampshire (2004, April).

INSTRUCTIONAL METHODOLOGIES

Universal Design for Learning (UDL)

UDL suggests that teachers proactively set up the learning environment and the activities in order to support the majority of the children in the classroom. First, children with ASD can have challenges *engaging* with the physical activity program. This relates to setting up a program that supports interest, effort, and persistence (Center for Applied Special Technology, 2011). Supports include:

- Following a consistent schedule of activities each session
- Creating and maintaining motivation
- Supporting transitions during the program
- Creating a set of routines and procedures

From the start, teachers should set up the environment in ways that are likely to provide these supports for children with ASD. This would include limiting the number of activities that children complete during each session of the program. This strategy will reduce the number of transitions, and keep the schedule as consistent as possible. Each session should run in a predictable way so that children with ASD can get into the flow and will be more likely to participate successfully.

Second, children with ASD can have trouble learning new material during the day. This relates to *representation* in UDL, or considering how information is shared with learners. Supports include:

- Understanding how to perform specific skills, such as catching or throwing
- Helping children understand the expectations of each activity
- Helping children learn the routine and procedures used during the program

These goals will be supported through strategies suggested below in the discussion of visual supports, and modeling and guided practice.

Activity Schedules

Teachers should create a schedule for children with ASD for the physical activity program. This will help children understand the flow of the program and help get them involved. The schedule should include each of the main activities you plan to include that day, such as a relay race or practicing the skill of the day. Decide how your children are best able to access the schedule. Some children may be able to follow a class schedule, while others will need an individualized one. The physical activity program should be added to the daily schedule. Using a mini-schedule of all the activities that will be used in the physical activity program can also help children adapt to the flow.

The best way to develop an activity schedule may be using Boardmaker (Mayer-Johnson, Inc., 2011) software for the picture symbols, but not all teachers will have access to this program. You could also take pictures of the equipment, children using the equipment, or children engaging in activities such as throwing, catching, or kicking. Better yet, a video of a child performing activities such as throwing and catching a ball could be very effective. Teachers could also access websites for resources and pictures for an activity schedule. Suggested websites are included at the end of chapter 5.

Repeating activities can help children with ASD. For example, keep the exercise portion of the program consistent by only including a few options for exercise in each session. Find exercises that your class likes, and repeat them. Have one or two exercise activities that you always use on indoor days or outdoor days. The motor development portion of the program will have more variability, since you'll have children practicing new skills each week or every two weeks.

Priming

Teachers should consider ways to "prime" children prior to the start of the physical activity program (Koegel, Koegel, Frea, & Green-Hopkins, 2003). You can review previous activities, introduce new concepts, or share any changes in the schedule. Priming can include:

- Sending materials home
- Practicing activities prior to the program starting

- Reviewing the activities before they are used in the program (this could occur the day before, or anytime in the day prior to the start of the program)

Teachers should also use visuals, videos, or modeling during priming, when possible. This could be done as a whole class or during an activity such as "morning meeting," but teachers should keep a close eye on children with ASD, in case they need additional support. See textbox 4.1 for a few simple steps teachers can follow during the priming session.

TEXTBOX 4.1.
Steps for implementing a priming session

Step 1: Review the activities that the class will be completing during the physical activity program that day (or the next day, if you choose to do this at the end of the school day). Refer to the visual schedule for the program.
Step 2: Check to see if students have any questions as you discuss each activity. Try to help them understand what is expected to perform selected motor and social skills. Use modeling and guided practice to support these skills.
Step 3: Review a Social Story or script that targets appropriate behaviors to use during the physical activity program.
Step 4: Check to see if children can repeat back what you will be doing that day, and what motor or social skills they should be focusing on.
Step 5: Repeat steps if necessary.

Visual Supports

Include pictures of activities, when possible. This could include pictures of specific children or their peers completing activities. Use visual supports (e.g., picture task cards, activity schedules, images or videos of activities, physical demonstrations) as a way to minimize the use of verbal instruction. This can include picture task cards that are paired with physical demonstrations of activities. A visual timer (for example a Time Timer or online timer) may also help children understand how long each activity will take. Finally, videos can work well to show children how to perform specific activities. See the Resources Section at the end of chapter 5 for additional information.

Modeling and Guided Practice

Teachers should take time to consider and explicitly review how children will perform each activity. Remember to pace this based on your children's receptive language processing. Practice each activity, and demonstrate how they should perform it. Adding visual supports will make this instruction clearer. One way to add visual guidance is through a version of "I Do, We Do, You Do." Modeling and guided practice can involve five steps:

1. *State the objective and purpose*: Teachers should state what they will be practicing during the program that day (e.g., throwing with one hand) and try to explain why this is important (e.g., playing catch with friends during recess can be fun, and this skill is needed for games like baseball). This will help children know what to expect that day and why this is important to learn. Reducing the number of activities you do during each session, and repeating these activities, will reduce the need for you to practice and teach new activities. Children with ASD are frequently happy to repeat activities they enjoy, and they gain confidence through this repeated practice.
2. *Model the skill*: Teachers should clearly model how to perform the skill, and use the same materials the children will use, such as floor markers for foot placement and balls. The skills and some activities will be described in more detail in chapter 5. Teachers can show children the motions they will use, and verbalize each step. Chapter 5 also contains illustrations of some skills, such as throwing with one hand. Finally, it may be helpful to ask for volunteers to come up to model the skill. This can be fun and motivating for children, and provides an additional model for them.
3. *Check for understanding*: Make sure students understand what is expected. You can ask for questions, or ask them probing questions. For example, ask questions like, "Where do my feet go when I'm throwing the ball?" or "Where do I look when I throw?"

4. *Guided practice*: Give children a chance to practice the skills. This can be done as a whole class, in small groups, or by having children come up and try out the skill individually. Keep kids as engaged as possible during guided and independent practice, so they get more practice time and stay involved. Providing a chance to use the equipment can help familiarize them with the materials and expectations. Rotate between children, and support as needed. Some practice can also take place during priming sessions or by sending materials home.
5. *Independent practice*: Children can get additional practice with activities through independent practice in pairs or small groups. Teachers should rotate around to provide support as needed. Independent practice can also occur by adding extra activities into obstacle courses (e.g., a station that has children using a one-handed throw to a put a ball or beanbag through a hoop) or by encouraging children to practice the skills of the week on the playground or at home.

Finally, use a system of least-to-most prompts as you work with children on different tasks (Neitzel & Wolery, 2009). In this system, teachers provide help as needed to children during different activities throughout the program. In general, children will require more support as they first learn how to perform an activity or skill, and less support as they develop proficiency and their comfort level increases. The hierarchy has several levels. The first is no prompts, or independent level. This is the ultimate goal. Other levels of support include:

1. Verbal: This involves using language, such as "kick the ball," "feet on floor markers," and "look at your partner." One caution: verbal support can be difficult to fade; therefore, teachers may try to use gestural or visual prompts more frequently.
2. Gestural: This involves using gestures, such as pointing, to help children know what to do next. Visual supports also work well here (holding up a picture and pointing to the action or skill).
3. Modeling: This was described above in detail. Teachers can also quickly model for children who forget a skill or specific steps. This can involve quick prompts, such "do this" and "look at me" (as the teacher models the specific skill).

4. Physical (partial and full): This involves using hand-over-hand support to help a child understand how to move his or her body to perform the skill. Help a child only as much as they need to complete the skill, and work on fading this support over time. For example, a teacher may show a child a one-handed throw by taking their hand through the motions and helping them release the ball. As the child gets more skilled, the teacher can use a lighter touch, and then simply touching their wrist or elbow to cue the correct motion.

Routines and Procedures

Children with ASD need consistent expectations throughout the day. Establishing routines and procedures during a physical activity program can support this. For example, establish routines for the overall program, such as always conducting the activities in the same place or having a set way to complete individual activities. It saves time to repeat activities in this way, and children will get used to the routine.

Procedures can be established for parts of the program, such as cleanup. Repeating lessons or activities also seems to help children get into the flow of the program and perform better (Schultheis, Boswell, & Decker, 2000). For example, try to run the activity program the same way for the first few days, and then add some variation. This way the children can get into the flow and know what to expect. You could also create a routine for how the area looks, such as designated spots for activities or "wait chairs" for children to use in between activities. If possible, establish a set time in the day and/or week to conduct the program.

Social Narratives

Social narratives describe situations by focusing on relevant cues and providing examples of appropriate responses (Wong et al., 2013). Social narratives are individualized, written in the first person from the child's perspective, and can be short. They may also contain pictures or other visual supports. The narratives should describe the situation, provide suggestions for appropriate behaviors, and describe the perspectives of others involved, such as teachers or peers. The social narrative can help describe the expectations for the physical activity program and prepare children for participation.

Teachers can use the social narrative to focus on particular goals or areas of concern, such as why they are doing certain activities or engaging in different behaviors. Social Stories (Gray, 2004) are one type of social narrative. Each story attempts to describe a situation and expectations clearly and accurately. The stories often include the expectations of others who are involved, such as peers and teachers. See textbox 4.2 for an example social narrative about waiting for your turn.

TEXTBOX 4.2.
Social narrative: Waiting for my turn

We play games in school. Sometimes during games and activities, I need to wait for my turn. This means that I sit or stand quietly. I wait for my teacher to tell me it's my turn. This will make my teacher happy, and will help everyone have more turns. I will also try to watch my classmates when they have a turn. I can cheer for them by saying "great job" or "nice throw." This will make my classmates happy. Everyone likes to get cheered for during a game.

Social Stories and social narratives can also be used to target specific social behaviors. More information on how to write a Social Story will be presented in chapter 6.

OTHER CONSIDERATIONS

Reinforcement

Some of the children in your program may need additional reinforcement to participate, but experience has demonstrated that the activities are reinforcing for them. This is especially true when you select activities the kids like; as they gain confidence, they will successfully complete new skills. Use positive reinforcement (such as cheers, smiles, and high-fives) and try to choose activities that kids enjoy so that they are naturally reinforcing. One idea is to allow kids to choose activities, if they are choosing from a list that focuses on your target goals. This choice tends to be reinforcing, and therefore increases motivation.

Special Interests

Another way to create motivation and engagement is by including activities, when possible, that are connected to a child's special interest. For example, teachers can look to find ways to connect to games the child already enjoys, such as baseball or football. The Power Card Strategy (see, e.g., Keeling, Smith-Myles, Gagnon, & Simpson, 2003) utilizes a card based on a child's specific interest or hero that describes how the hero has used the strategy successfully and encourages the child to try it as well.

Sensory Issues

Teachers should be aware of potential sensory issues of their students, and try to account for these when running the physical activity program. Get to know your students and how they respond to certain environments or senses. For example, many children with ASD will be sensitive to sights or sounds that occur in different places. Use this knowledge as you think about where you will conduct the program. Walk around the space you plan to use, and consider potential factors such as the time of day you will use that space.

Priming or working to prepare children for the activities may reduce negative sensory responses. Children may also just adapt to an environment over time. When implementing a motor skills program in one school, teachers conducted it in a common area that saw a lot of traffic throughout the day. Many were concerned that the space would be too distracting, and it was, at first, for some of the children. Over time, though, the children became used to the space, and as they became more engaged in the program, they were less distracted by people walking past them. This ability to focus is actually a great skill to learn.

TAKEAWAYS

1. Teachers should consider key areas, such as structure and setting, as they plan for a physical activity program.
2. Settings should meet the needs of the children and can vary based on spaces available in the school.

3. Evidence-based interventions (e.g., priming, narratives, visuals) can easily be embedded in physical activity programs and individualized based on kids' needs.
4. Group configurations are flexible when implementing physical activity programs. Be sure to consider children's needs, and how teachers and volunteers can be utilized to assist to enhance skill attainment.

REFERENCES

Case-Smith, J., & O'Brien, J. C. (2010). *Occupational therapy for children.* Maryland Heights, MD: Elsevier.

Center for Applied Special Technology (CAST). (2011). *Universal design for learning guidelines, version 2.0.* Wakefield, MA: Author.

Gray, C. (2004). Social Stories 10.0: The new defining criteria and guidelines. *Jenison Autism Journal, 15,* 1–26.

Keeling, K., Smith-Myles, B., Gagnon, E., & Simpson, R. L. (2003). Using the Power Card Strategy to teach sportsmanship skills to a child with autism. *Focus on Autism and Other Developmental Disabilities, 18*(2), 103–9.

Koegel, L. K., Koegel, R. L., Frea, W., & Green-Hopkins, I. (2003). Priming as a method of coordinating educational services for students with autism. *Language, Speech, & Hearing Services in Schools, 34,* 228–35.

Mayer-Johnson, Inc. (2011). *Boardmaker, version 6.* Solana Beach, CA: Author.

National Association for Sport and Physical Education. (2009). *Active Start* (2nd ed.). Oxon Hill, MD: AAHPERD Publications.

National Institute of Health. (2011). *Normal growth and development.* Retrieved from http://www.nlm.nih.gov/medlineplus/ency/article/002456.htm

Neitzel, J., & Wolery, M. (2009). *Steps for implementation: Least to most prompts.* Chapel Hill, NC: National Professional Development Center on Autism Spectrum Disorder, Frank Porter Graham Child Development Institute, University of North Carolina.

Schultheis, S. F., Boswell, B. B., & Decker, J. (2000). Successful physical activity programming for students with autism. *Focus on Autism and Other Developmental Disabilities, 15,* 159–62.

University of New Hampshire. (2004, April). *The 3, 4 and 5-year-old: Physical changes.* Retrieved from: http://extension.unh.edu/family/documents/ec345_phys.pdf

U.S. Department of Health & Human Services. (2008). *Physical activity guidelines for Americans.* Washington, DC: Author.

Wong, C., Odom, S. L., Hume, K. Cox, A. W., Fettig, A., Kucharczyk, S., et al. (2013). *Evidence-based practices for children, youth, and young adults with Autism Spectrum Disorder.* Chapel Hill, NC: Frank Porter Graham Child Development Institute, Autism Evidence-Based Practice Review Group, University of North Carolina.

5

THE PHYSICAL ACTIVITY PROGRAM

This chapter is organized into three parts. The first section describes the key components that should be part of a physical activity program. These include: (a) exercise, (b) motor skill development, and (c) a cool down period. The second section provides examples of activities teachers can use during each section. This will be presented, in part, like an à la carte menu. The third section will provide an overview of published programs that contain all or most of these components.

There are a number of key points to consider as you start a physical activity program. These were discussed in chapter 2 and will be reviewed briefly here. First, children (and adults) seem to benefit from engaging in both physical activity and complex motor movements during the day (Klintsova, Dickson, Yoshida, & Greenough, 2004).

Second, children seem to benefit from the increased levels of BDNF that occur during physical activity and this effect is enhanced when we add complex motor movements. Benefits include increased rates of learning and improved executive functioning skills (e.g., attention and wait time). In fact, John Ratey (2008) referred to BDNF as "Miracle Gro for the brain" (p. 42) due to its role in helping to build, strengthen, and maintain brain connections. Third, physical activity increases levels of neurotransmitters such as serotonin, norepinephrine, and dopamine that result in improved attention, mood, and motivation, and decreased anxiety and aggression.

The physical activity program should contain three main components:

- Aerobic exercise or physical activity
- Motor development or complex motor movements
- Cool down or meditation

WHAT DOES IT LOOK LIKE?

Aerobic Exercise or Physical Activity

First, kids should engage in aerobic exercise that lasts for at least 10 minutes. Exercise is defined as "a form of physical activity that is planned, structured, repetitive and performed with the goal of improving health or fitness" (U.S. Department of Health and Human Services, 2008, p. 7). Exercise should also raise children's heart rates. If possible, track heart rates during this time so that they are at 60–70 percent of maximum. To calculate maximum heart rate, subtract the child's age from 220. Thus, the maximum heart rate for a five-year-old should be 215 beats per minute, and 60–80 percent of maximum would be 129–172 beats per minute. When you are just starting a program, you could set a target rate at 50 percent or 107 beats per minute for a five-year-old child ("Target Heart Rates," 2015). You can also check heart rates using a wristband, such as a Fitbit, or by teaching children how to find their own heart rate in one of two places. The neck seems to be the easiest place to take a pulse. First, teach children to place two or three fingers on their Adam's apple (the bump at the front of the neck). Once located, have the child shift his or her fingers to either side, to feel a beat or pulsing. (Teachers should try to find their pulse on their own necks.) Next, have the children count the number of beats they feel in 10 seconds. Finally, have them multiply by 6 or tell someone the number so they can multiply. It may be easier to have children count for 6 seconds, tell you the number, and then multiply by 10.

Motor Development and Complex Motor Movements

Next, children should practice complex motor movements for 10–15 minutes. This can include activities such as an obstacle course, games, activities, or yoga. You should also determine focus areas each week (such as throwing or catching) based on a developmental progression or need.

Meditation or Calming Activity

Finally, a calming or meditation component should last for 5–10 minutes. This helps children refocus and get ready to learn again. Activities could include breath work, yoga (such as Kripalu yoga), or stretching.

HOW CAN I DO IT?

Aerobic Exercise or Physical Activity (Part 1)

There are a number of ways to have children engage in physical activity. Teachers could choose activities that last for 10–15 minutes straight, or a series of activities that add up to 10–15 minutes. This depends on how your children respond to different activities. It may be better to have one activity that lasts for the entire time. Children with ASD tend to struggle with transitions, so if you just have one activity, then you don't need to deal with a transition.

Children with ASD also tend to like repeating activities, especially once they get the hang of a skill, so you may not need to come up with too many ways to engage in the exercise component. The key is to make it fun and engaging, and to get heart rates up. The children should enjoy all the activities that you do. Therefore, it is important to add choice as a component, so that when you find an activity they like, you can add it to your list of options (or choice board) and always have it available as an option. Some children may be very happy doing the same activity over and over again, and some will want some level of variation. Some may require adult support, and some children may be able to participate independently.

Suggestions for Physical Activity/Aerobic Exercise

- Jumping rope (many kids with ASD may not be able to jump rope in the traditional way, so it may be necessary to scaffold the skills needed for jumping rope)

  - First, have children practice jumping over a rope that is on the ground.
  - Next, have children practice walking and stepping over the rope. The rope would make a complete rotation over their body, but they would step over it (rather than jump over it). As they get more skilled they can speed up the rotation and begin to jump over the rope.
  - Children can practice jumping and walking over the rope as part of the motor development activities, and then use jumping rope as an exercise activity once kids get the hang of it.
- Jumping in place
- Trampoline
  - Jump a set number of times.
- Swinging
- Running
  - This could occur in the hallway, back and forth in a space like the gym or blacktop area, or run in place, or on an outdoor track. Weave in and out of cones.
- Relay race
  - Have kids perform any form of movement that raises heart rates and keeps them active.
  - Animal walks: crab, bear, or slither like a snake. All of these are great for weight bearing through the hands to develop upper body and core strength.
  - Zoom or speed ball with a partner. This promotes coordination and crossing midline.
- Playing tag or other chase games
- Bouncy ball: throw and catch to self a set number of times, pass back and forth with a partner, or pass ball over and under with a line of students.
- Therapy ball: bounce-pass back and forth with a starting point of holding the ball overhead, roll the ball back and forth with a partner, or roll it individually for a certain distance.
- Scooter: children can lie down or sit on a scooter board and propel themselves using their arms or legs.
- Skipping, galloping, hopping, or walking forward or backward
- Dancing

- Yoga, and holding yoga positions
- Trail walking or hiking
- Swimming
- Biking or stationary biking
- Rollerblading

Motor Development and Complex Motor Movements (Part 2)

Teachers can focus on motor development in many ways. Some teachers prefer to help their children master a skill before progressing to the next skill. Others are comfortable with practicing a skill or set of skills for a few weeks, and then progressing to a new set of skills. It is important for children to be able to imitate motor movements, so imitation is an early area of focus. Textbox 5.1 presents one way to organize your units to work on key motor development skills.

TEXTBOX 5.1.
Model schedule for a physical activity program

Unit	*Skill Focus*
Unit 1	Foundational skills
Unit 2	Walking and running
Unit 3	Jumping
Unit 4	Throwing
Unit 5	Catching
Unit 6	Kicking
Unit 7	Trapping
Unit 8	Striking

All of the target areas in textbox 5.1 relate to skills discussed below. Stationary skills are addressed in unit 1, foundational skills (e.g., balance, visual tracking). Locomotion skills are addressed in units 2 and 3 (e.g., walking, running, and jumping). Lastly, object manipulation skills are addressed in units 4 through 8 (e.g., throwing, catching, kicking, trapping, and striking).

Activities for Motor Development and Complex Motor Movements

This section provides an overview of each area and contains a description of each skill and helpful tips to make it easier to practice these skills with your students. Two tables below describe the key steps involved in performing each skill. In addition, a series of figures illustrate many of the motor movements. Finally, suggested activities for practicing each skill are listed.

The first area to consider is *stationary skills* or *foundational skills*. This includes working on key areas such as balance (e.g., standing on one foot or walking on a balance beam) and core body strength (e.g., yoga poses or sit-ups).

Imitation involves copying peers or adults. This is an important skill throughout the school day and crucial during the physical activity program, since children will need to copy their teacher or peers to learn how to complete new skills. Ways to include imitation:

- "Simon Says."
- Dancing (for variety, have each child teach a dance move).
- Clapping games: clap hands on body parts, encourage midline crossing.

Visual tracking includes skills that involve watching a ball as a child prepares to catch it, watching a peer as a child prepares to throw the ball, and knowing where peers are during games, such as soccer or tag. Ways to include visual tracking:

- Throw scarves into the air and then catch them.
- Try to catch or pop bubbles.
- Try to keep a balloon or ball in the air (this can be played alone or with a partner). For variety, children can use a paddle to keep a balloon in the air.

Crossing midline involves reaching across the middle of the body with the arms or legs. Crossing midline involves using hands or feet to perform a task on the opposite side of the body, such as using the right hand to catch a ball on the left side of the body. Ways to include midline crossing:

- Walk or march in a straight line, touching each knee or thigh with the opposite hand (e.g., touch the right knee with the left hand).
- Stand still and touch the elbow to the opposite knee.
- Practice drawing a diagonal line on a page (e.g., top left to bottom right).
- ABC push-ups: Children hold a plank and tap opposite shoulder with hands while saying the alphabet (they can go to their knees if the plank is too difficult or when they get tired).
- Other activities connected with crossing midline, such as clapping games.

Balance for children includes skills such as kneeling, standing on one foot or tiptoes, and walking on a balance beam. There are multiple types of balance beams to use. A fabric beam can be purchased and taped down, if needed, to create more stability. You can make a balance beam using a 2 x 4 board, or masking or duct tape, or even chalk on the playground.

Teachers can differentiate skills on the beam. One way is to have children walk with one foot on the beam and the other foot on the floor, and gradually take more steps that include both feet on the beam. Ways to include balance:

- Use balance beams at individual activity stations, during one-on-one activities, or embedded into activities such as an obstacle course.
- Walk forward, backward, or sideways on the balance beam.
- Create games with the beam by having children pretend it is a log that helps them cross a pond or river.
- Walk along the balance beam carrying a ball or object (try holding it first, then walking while throwing and catching.
- Jump over or jump on and off the beam.
- Walk on edges or step into middle of tires or hoops.
- Step over a mat, brick, or hose.
- Practice balancing on many items; for example, a walk in the woods or a path that includes rocks or logs that children must walk or jump across (an outdoor obstacle course).
- Swinging helps develop balance and coordination as children shift their weight and pump their legs.

- Dancing (hold poses).
- Create or use balance boards; these often include a maze on top that must be completed using a golf or ping-pong ball.

Core strength for children includes yoga poses, sit-ups, and push-ups. There are multiple ways for teachers to think about core strength. This area involves building up endurance and strength so children can more easily perform more complicated gross motor movements. Children can make significant gains in this area with consistent and repeated practice.

Favazza, Zeisel, Parker, and Leboeuf (2011) used the idea of bridges and tunnels in the Young Athletes Program to help children build core strength, especially upper-body strength. These ideas are connected to yoga poses, such as downward dog, and can also be incorporated into the cool down section. The "bridge" that children form looks like the downward dog position in yoga. More than one child performing the skill side by side would produce a "tunnel." When the bridge or tunnel is formed, children can then crawl underneath in the case of the bridge, or through in the case of the tunnel. Children really seemed to enjoy this. It is difficult for many at first, but they can improve rapidly with practice. It is also motivating and fun for them to hold the position while their peers crawl under. Ways to include core strength:

- Practice individually to see how long children can hold a position.
- Work with partners and take turns acting as the bridge or the tunnel.
- Multiple children can work together to create a tunnel and then take turns crawling through.
- Practice by leaning up against a wall.
- Practice by rolling other objects under the bridge, such as a ball or car.

The second skill area to consider is *locomotion*. This includes working on key areas such as running, skipping, or jumping. It's important for teachers to understand how to teach specific skills and what to focus on for children to be successful. See table 5.1 for a description of what teachers should consider when teaching each skill. Demonstrating the performance of these skills works well, or have specific children demonstrate for the class. Figures correspond to the descriptions in table 5.1 and are presented throughout the chapter. Teachers can use the guidelines to track and support performance during guided and independent practice opportunities.

Table 5.1. Performance criteria for locomotion skills

Locomotion Skill	*Performance Criteria*
Run	• Move arms opposite to legs, and bend arms. • Both feet are off the ground for some period of time. • Land on heel or toe first, and then rest of foot comes down. Should not land flat-footed. • Support leg is bent on landing. Non-support leg is bent 90 degrees or more.
Gallop	• Bend arms so hands are near waist level at takeoff. • Hop forward with lead foot and then quickly bring trailing foot to a position adjacent to or behind the lead foot. • Both feet are off the ground for some period of time. • Repeat for as many cycles as possible. Lead foot stays in the lead.
Skip	• Essentially a series of hops (looks like *step-hop-step-hop*). • Flex arms and swing them forward to create power. • Bend support leg. • Keep non-support leg bent, with foot behind body. • Swing non-support leg to create power for hop. • Step forward and repeat steps with other leg. • Repeat sequence.
Slide	• Turn body sideways and keep toes facing forward. • Slide one foot to the left or right. • Bring other foot next to lead foot. • Repeat.
Horizontal jump (two feet)	• Prepare to jump by bending knees slightly and extending arms behind body. • For takeoff, reach arms forward or upward until they extend over your head. • Takeoff and land on both feet simultaneously. • During landing, arms come forward and knees bend deeply.
Leap (one foot)	• Lead with one foot and land on the opposite foot. • Both feet are off the ground during the jump. • Reach forward with arm opposite the lead foot.
Hop (on one foot)	• Flex arms and swing them forward to create power. • Bend support leg. • Keep non-support leg bent, with foot behind body. • Swing non-support leg to create power for hop. • Practice on both preferred and non-preferred feet.

Source: Adapted from Alhassan et al., 2012.

Walking and *running* includes such skills as skipping, galloping, walking forward and backward, running forward or backward, using scooter boards, and walking up and down stairs. Figure 5.1 illustrates body positioning for running, and figures 5.2 and 5.3 depict positions for skipping.

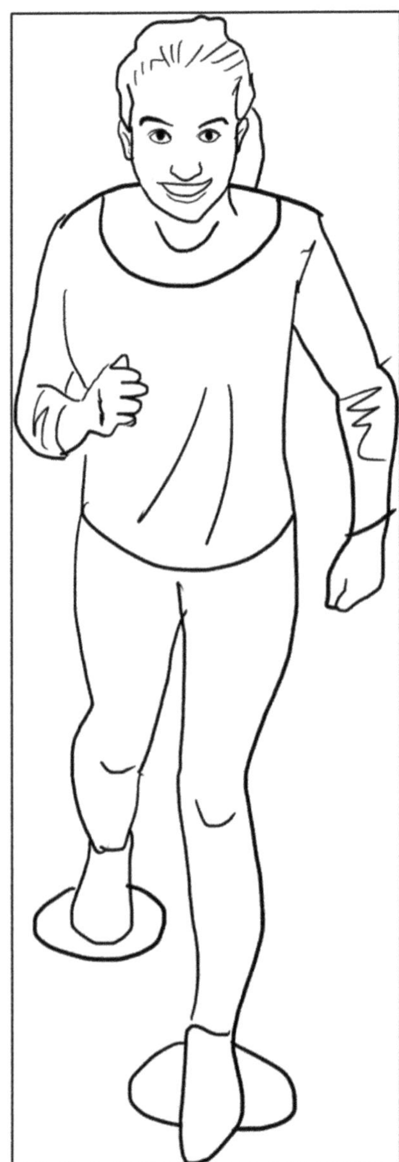

Figure 5.1. Run

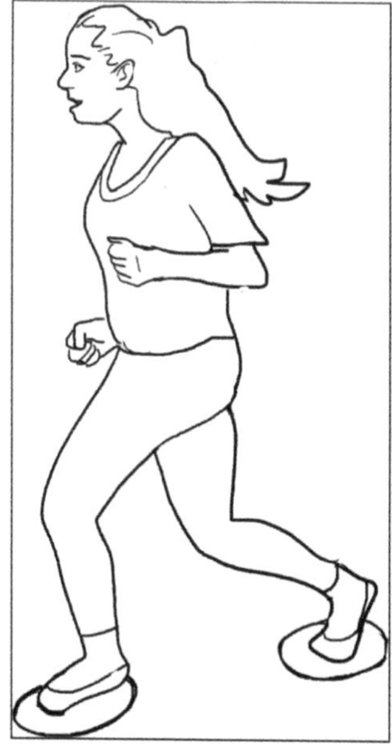

Figure 5.2. Skip: 1

Figure 5.3. Skip: 2

There are multiple ways for teachers to vary walking and running for children. A progression of skills for walking and running includes walking forward, backward, and sidestepping (or slide stepping), to running forward and backward, and then more complicated movements such as skipping and galloping. These can all be practiced in a variety of ways, including utilizing stairs, hallways, and open spaces, or creating relay races and obstacle courses.

Children enjoy practicing these activities by taking turns down the hallway or across the gym and playground. The class can practice specific skills, or the teacher can vary the activity by calling out changes for each group or even having the groups change skills in the middle of an activity. For example, the teacher could start a group with skipping, and then blow the whistle to change to another skill, such as hopping or running backward. These activities can be non-competitive or competitive. Teachers can even add additional skills, such as pairing students for wheelbarrow walking or having children practice various animal walks such as bear, bunny, or crab walking. Adding music can also increase movement. Ways to include walking and running:

- Practice different running styles such as running slow and fast, walking and running backward, stomping slow and fast, tiptoe walking, and high knees walking/running. This could be done as relay races, taking turns, or embedded into an obstacle course.
- Sidestepping: use floor markers to show where to go, and practice on a taped line, balance beam, or along a jump rope.

Jumping includes skills such as jumping in place, hopping on one foot, jumping on and off objects, and one- and two-footed short leaps and long jumps. Figures 5.4 to 5.9 illustrate body positioning for horizontal jumps, leaps, and hops.

There are multiple ways for teachers to vary jumping for children. One consideration is to have children practice jumping with two feet. This builds explosive power and leg strength. Explore ways to vary the height and length of jumps. Height can be varied by having children jump over, onto, and off objects, such as blocks and other sturdy platforms. Use Velcro to create platform or object stability, or have children jump off a non-skid surface to support safety and stability. Floor markers or tape on the floor can work as targets for jumping. Hurdles can be used to adjust for jumping height, or different playground equipment might provide varying heights for jumping off or over.

Figure 5.4. Horizontal jump: Ready

Figure 5.5. Horizontal jump: Finished

Figure 5.6. Leap: Ready

Figure 5.7. Leap: Finished

Figure 5.8. Hop: Ready

Figure 5.9. Hop: Finished

These are all ways to differentiate for varying skill levels in your group. For example, set up two hurdles of different heights to jump over. Children can choose one or the other so that everyone has the opportunity to experience success, and they can build on previous skills. Jumping can also be embedded into activities like an obstacle course, relay race, or other activities. Ways to include jumping:

- Practice jumping in different ways (one foot, two foot, side jump, over objects, off objects).
- Practice jumping as animals, like a bunny or frog.
- Use soft hurdles or cones (bricks) and bars to create hurdles.

The third area to consider is *object manipulation*. This includes key skills such as throwing, catching, and striking. It's important for teachers to understand how to teach specific skills and what to focus on for children to be successful. See table 5.2 for descriptions of what teachers should consider when teaching each skill, and see the figures that depict how children should look during the performance of each skill. Teachers can demonstrate the performance of these skills or have specific children demonstrate for the class, and then use the guidelines to track and support performance. Teachers can also use visual images to show children how they should look during specific skill performance.

Table 5.2. Performance criteria for object manipulation skills

Object Manipulation Skill	*Performance Criteria*
Overhand throw (two hands)	• Prepare for throw by stepping forward with non-dominant foot, bending knees slightly. • Point toes of front foot toward target (floor markers can be used to show foot placement). • Take ball in two hands and reach behind head. • Thrust arms forward and release ball when hands are directly overhead (or slightly forward). • Arms continue forward and rest at side. • Children can also step forward as they throw to create more stability.

Object Manipulation Skill	*Performance Criteria*
Underhand throw (one hand)	• Prepare for throw by stepping forward with non-dominant foot, bending knees slightly. • Point toes of front foot toward target. • Feet should be hip distance apart (floor markers can be used to show foot placement). • Take ball in dominant hand and reach behind thigh. Keep hand close to body. • Thrust arm forward and release ball when hand is just past thigh. • Hand continues forward and then comes back to side.
Overhand throw (one hand)	• Prepare to throw by stepping forward with non-dominant foot, bending knees slightly. • Point toes of front foot toward target (floor markers can be used to show foot placement). • Take ball in dominant hand and reach behind head close to ear. • Thrust arm forward and shift weight to forward foot. • Release ball when hand is just past head (about 11 o'clock). • Hand comes forward and rests at side.
Catch (two hands)	• Reach out with both hands at chest height and keep arms slightly bent. • Keep feet shoulder width apart. • Watch ball in the air and move hands toward ball. • Once ball touches hands, bring hands back toward chest so ball is trapped between arms and chest.
Catch (one hand)	• Reach out with preferred hand at chest height and keep arm slightly bent. • Keep feet shoulder width apart. • Watch ball in the air and move hand toward ball. • Once ball touches hand, bring hand back toward body.
Kick	• Face partner. • Stand with legs slightly bent and shoulder width apart. • Bring dominant foot back and bend knee. • Swing foot forward and make contact with ball with inside of foot or shoelaces (better to make contact with laces than with toe—"Say no to the toe").
Trap	• Stand facing partner. • Stand with legs slightly bent and shoulder width apart. • Turn foot with toes out as ball approaches, and trap ball with instep of foot.
Strike	• Stand sideways with non-dominant shoulder closest to target. • Hold the bat with the non-dominant hand closest to the bottom of the bat. • Bend arms and hold bat over shoulder. • Swing bat at ball on "T" or as ball approaches (when thrown) to make contact. • Finish swing with bat over other shoulder and continue holding onto bat.

Throwing can be underhand or overhand, and can involve one or two hands. There are multiple areas to consider during throwing activities. Figures 5.10 to 5.15 illustrate body positioning for overhand and underhand throws.

Figure 5.10. Overhand throw with two hands: Ready

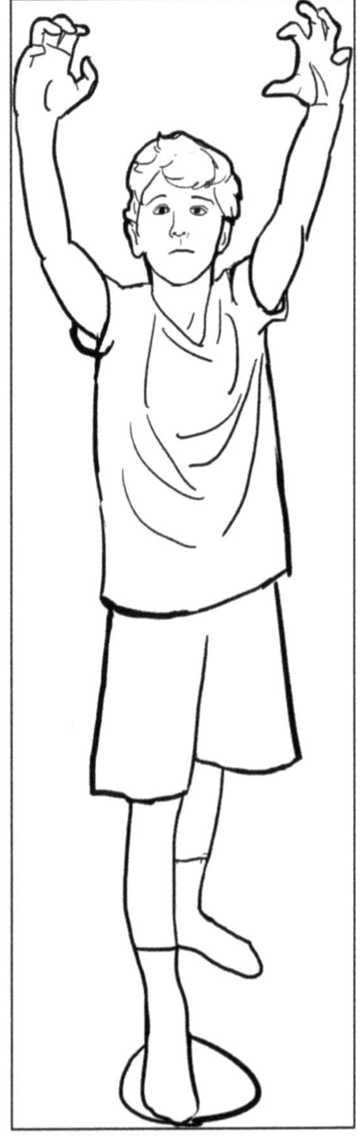

Figure 5.11. Overhand throw with two hands: Finished

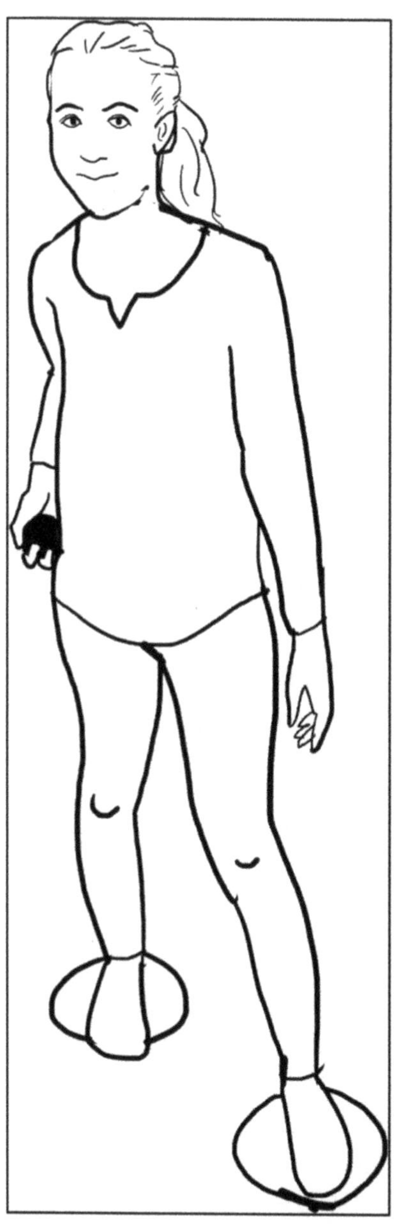

Figure 5.12. Underhand throw with one hand: Ready

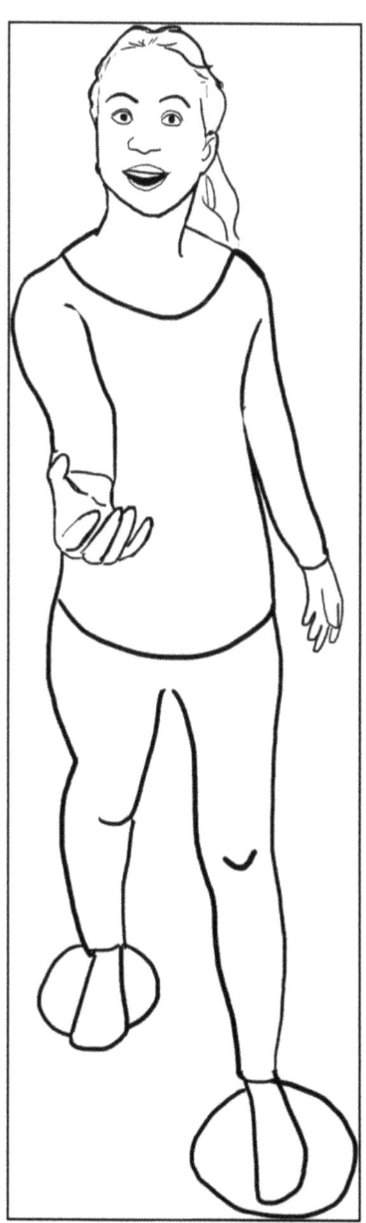

Figure 5.13. Underhand throw with one hand: Finished

Figure 5.14. Overhand throw with one hand: Ready

Figure 5.15. Overhand throw with one hand: Finished

Teachers should help children understand the difference between overhand and underhand throws. This may be a difficult concept for some kids. Many children may need additional support through partial or full hand-over-hand prompting to get the feel of both overhand and underhand throws. Underhand throws may be easier for children to perform, but it depends on the child. See figures 5.10 to 5.15 for illustrations demonstrating preparation for one-handed and two-handed throws and body positions during follow through. These pictures can be used alongside direct instruction to help illustrate how to perform these skills.

When working on throwing, teachers should create a target for children for each type of throw. This could include a hoop or materials from the classroom, such as boxes, baskets, buckets, targets made on a wall with tape, or targets made on the blacktop with chalk. Making this into a game could be fun for kids.

Teachers can also have children throw a variety of objects, depending upon the environment (inside or outside) or purpose of the activity. For example, throwing beanbags can be helpful, since they tend to stay where they land and are therefore easier to retrieve.

Teachers can differentiate in multiple ways. For example, if you create a station where children stand on a floor marker and throw a beanbag through a hoop, then children can take a step forward to make it easier and a step backward to make it more challenging. Ways to include throwing:

- Use Nerf balls, tennis balls, Wiffle balls, and small and large activity balls.
- Incorporate throwing into games like basketball, baseball, or football once kids have learned the skills in individual and small groups.
- Practice throwing for distance and accuracy.

Catching can involve one or both hands. There are multiple areas to consider with catching. Figures 5.16 to 5.19 illustrate body positioning for one and two-handed catches.

Figure 5.16. Two-handed catch: Ready

Figure 5.17. Two-handed catch: Finished

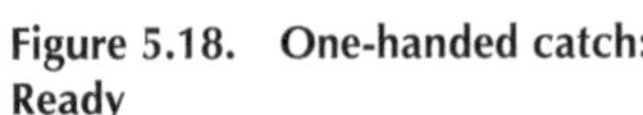

Figure 5.18. One-handed catch: Ready

Figure 5.19. One-handed catch: Finished

Children should practice with scarves, balloons, large balls, and then small balls (in that order). This helps with visually tracking the ball and gradually gaining confidence with catching.

Teachers may want to consider ball inflation as a way to help some of their children with ASD during catching activities. Balls that are underinflated may be easier for children to catch. This can be a useful way to differentiate for children as they first learn how to catch. The texture of some balls may also impact some children, and may offer multisensory exploration through trial and error. Balls that have some texture may be easier to catch than balls having a slippery or slick surface. Ways to include catching:

- Have children practice throwing a balloon in the air and catching it. Give a specific number of repeats for hitting the balloon and keeping it in the air.
- Have the child throw and catch the ball to him/herself by either throwing it in the air and catching it, or throwing it against the wall and catching it.
- Have the child hold a box or bucket with two hands to catch a ball thrown by a partner.
- Have children play games of catching and throwing to each other. Many kids are anxious about having a ball thrown to them; it might be best to start with children throwing to themselves.

Kicking involves hitting the ball with your foot. Figure 5.20 illustrates body positioning for kicks.

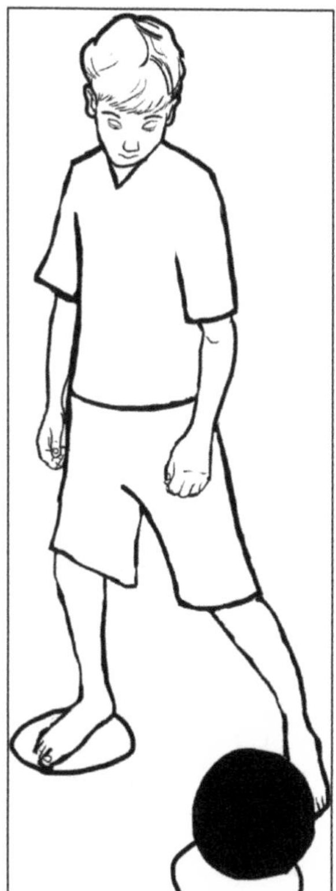

Figure 5.20. Kick

For kicking activities, modeling is important. Floor markers can work well to demonstrate foot placement for kicking. It is easier to start with kicking a still ball. In this case, teachers have children place their non-kicking foot on a floor marker that is beside the ball, and then bring the other foot forward to strike the ball. Ways to include kicking:

- Create games that involve targets (such as pins or water bottles) to aim at during kicking or goals to kick through.
- Practice kicking for distance and accuracy.
- Play kickball games.
- Practice scoring goals.
- Practice passing or "give and go."

Trapping involves stopping a ball with your foot. Figure 5.21 illustrates body positioning for trapping.

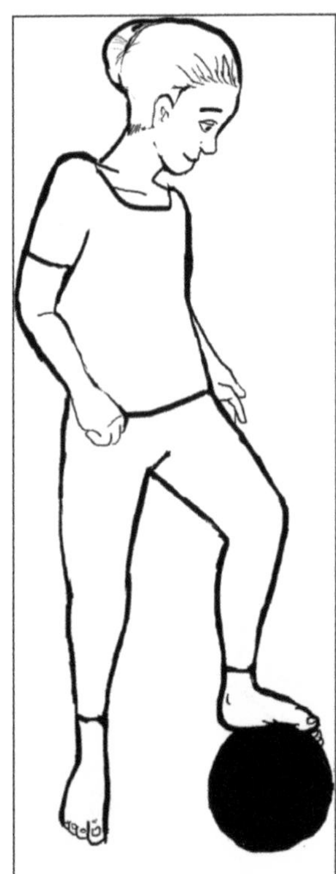

Figure 5.21. Trap

Ways to include trapping:

- Start young children on their knees, and roll the ball back and forth.
- Work with a partner and trap before you pass back. For variety, children can vary how far they stand apart.
- Kick ball against wall and then trap the ball on the return.

Striking involves hitting a ball with your hand or an instrument like a bat, racket, or stick. This can be done with one hand, or with both hands used together. There are multiple skills to consider during striking activities. Figures 5.22 and 5.23 illustrate body positioning for striking.

There are many ways to vary striking to differentiate for all learners and build skills. For example, vary the size of the bat to create a larger or smaller hitting surface. This includes using various rackets and bats. Vary the position of the ball by starting with the ball on some type of "tee," such as a cone, and then progress to pitching the ball to children as their skill and confidence level increase. Again, the adult may be simultaneously placing the ball on a tee for some children and pitching for others, since the abilities in student groups will vary.

Figure 5.22. Strike: Ready

Figure 5.23. Strike: Finished

You can also vary the type of ball that children are hitting. Start with larger and softer balls, and then gradually use smaller balls as their skills increase. It also may be helpful to start with balloons or large beach balls. Ways to include striking:

- Suspend a balloon on a string from the ceiling at eye-level height. Have students use a paper towel roll held bilaterally to practice hitting the balloon to reinforce visual tracking skills.
- Create different types of games and have children take roles such as batters and fielders.
- Play handball.
- Practice with a paddle, racket, hockey stick, or bat.

Meditation or Calming Activity (Part 3)

Experience suggests that children, especially children with ASD, need additional time and direct support in order to refocus and calm down prior to returning to classroom academic activities. Some kids get over-aroused during the exercise and motor development activities; therefore, a 5- to 10-minute cool down will help them, and the grownups involved, get ready for the next activity.

This can run as a whole-group activity. It also may work to have a few set ways that you get kids ready to transition to the next activity. Model for children how to perform each step as they verbalize the directions. Children will catch on to this activity and get more proficient during subsequent sessions.

Teachers can support children during the cool down in multiple ways. This includes visual supports, clear modeling during instruction, and guided practice with prompting, as needed. When working on activities that include focused breathing, it may help to use bubbles or pinwheels so children can see the effects, especially when these are first introduced.

Activities for Mediation or Calming

- Practice deep breathing.
- Practice calming activities, such as a yoga flow.

The activities described in table 5.3 could be conducted in multiple settings with small or large class sizes.

Table 5.3. Deep breathing examples

Activity	Teacher Directives
Description of directives	• Teacher states bulleted phrases below as directions to children. • Parenthetical phrases are optional, and are likely used the first few times children complete the activity. • Italicized phrases are directions for additional teacher explanations.
Deep breathing	• *Have children sit down.* • Close your eyes (or not). • Put one hand on your belly. • Put other hand on your heart. • Take a deep breath in through your nose and feel your hands rise. • Open your mouth and let your breath out. • Feel your hands fall. • Take another deep breath in and hold it. • Let out your breath as I count to three.
Flower and candle	• *Have children stand.* • Put your arms out to your side (like forming a letter T). • Pretend one hand is a flower (like a rose). *Teachers should talk about how nice the flower smells.* • Pretend the other hand holds a birthday candle. • Turn your head slowly to the rose and sniff. It's far away, so inhale strongly. • Turn to the other side and blow out the candle. • *Repeat three times.* • Put your hands down. • Close your eyes and count back from five.
Balloon belly	• *Have children stand.* • Put your hands on your belly. • Pretend that your stomach is a balloon. • Fill it with air by taking a deep breath in through your nose. • Hold it for three, two, and one. • Let it out slowly. Feel the balloon deflate. • *Repeat three times.*
Earth and sky	• *Have children stand.* • Bend down and tickle your toes. • Take a deep breath and slowly reach for the sky. • Tickle the birds. • As you exhale, bend back down to the earth and tickle the ants. • Take a deep breath in as you tickle yourself. • *Repeat three times.*

Eagle breath	• *Have children stand.*
	• Pretend you are a bird and your arms are wings.
	• Put your hands down by your side.
	• Take a deep breath in and have your wings float (lift or rise) up.
	• Take a deep breath out and have your wings float (fall) down by your side.
	• *Repeat five times.*
	• Close your eyes and imagine you're still flying above the trees.
	• Imagine you're flying through the clouds.
	• Visualize if you can . . .
	  ◦ Your body is light as a feather. Ahead of you are some fluffy white clouds. Below you are the fields and mountains. You are soaring above it all. (*Wait 30 seconds*).
	  ◦ Slowly you start to land. Once you land open your eyes. You can open your eyes in one, two, and three.

Teachers can also utilize an activity called a "flow." A flow is a series of movements or poses that follow each other. It can help increase awareness and focus on the breath. For the purposes of this book, the flow is intended to help kids regain focus and get ready for the next activity. See textbox 5.2 for an example of a flow that could be used at the end of a physical activity program. Teachers should model for children how to perform each step as they verbalize.

TEXTBOX 5.2.
Simple flow example: Tickle the sky, tickle the ground

Teacher Directives

1. Take a deep breath as you lift your arms up to tickle the sky.
2. Breathe out as you bend over with your legs straight and tickle the ground.
3. Keep your legs straight and tickle your knees.
4. Tickle the ground.
5. Bend your knees out to the side (squat).
6. Put your bottom on the ground and crisscross your legs.
7. Lift up your right hand to the sky and reach as high as you can.
8. Put that hand on your opposite (left) knee and place your other hand on the floor behind your back.
9. Look back.
10. Take a deep breath in and reach both arms to the sky.
11. Reach as high as you can.
12. Put both hands on floor.
13. Lift up your left hand to the sky and reach as high as you can.
14. Put that hand on your opposite (right) knee and place your other hand on the floor behind your back.
15. Look back.
16. Take a deep breath in and reach both arms to the sky.
17. Reach as high as you can.
18. Put both hands on floor.
19. Close your eyes while I count backward from 20.
20. Open your eyes and wait for the next direction.

WHERE CAN I GET MORE INFORMATION?

Resources for Exercise and Motor Development

PE Central: http://www.pecentral.org/

Provides physical education activities, ideas, and games for children in preschool, grades 3–5, grades 6–8, and grades 9–12. This online resource also offers various assessment and tracking tools for gathering student fitness information. Finally, the site provides information for teachers, classes, and online physical education programs.

Healthy Schools: http://www.cdc.gov/healthyschools/physicalactivity/guidelines.htm

Provides articles and information regarding to youth physical activity, and general recommendations for parents, schools, and communities. The *Physical Guidelines for Americans* is issued by the U.S. Department of Health and Human Services.

Go Noodle: www.gonoodle.com

Provides various activities to get kids moving in the classroom. Could be used to supplement activities in a physical activity program.

School Sparks: http://www.schoolsparks.com/early-childhood-development/gross-motor

Provides information regarding early childhood development and eight main developmental areas (fine motor development, auditory processing, visual discrimination, letter and word awareness, phonemic awareness, math and number awareness, social and emotional development, and gross motor development), and strategies to assess a child and foster his or her growth in each area.

Visual Supports

Picture Set: http://www.setbc.org/pictureSET/Default.aspx

Provides visual resources to use in the classroom during a physical activity program. Resources can be downloaded in multiple formats.

E-Learning Visuals: http://visuals.autism.net/main.php

Provides resources to use in the classroom during a physical activity program. Contains reproducible pictures, schedules, and demonstration videos.

TAKEAWAYS

1. Teachers should implement an activity program that includes three main components: (a) exercise, (b) motor development, and (c) cool down.
2. Teachers should strive for approximately 30 minutes of activity per day, three days per week, but how this time is allotted can be flexible.
3. Children with ASD may benefit from and seem to enjoy repeating activities during the physical activity program.
4. Every class and every student will have different needs.

REFERENCES

Alhassan, S., Nwaokelemeh, O., Ghazarian, M., Roberts, J., Mendoza, A., & Shitole, S. (2012). Effects of locomotor skill program on preschoolers' physical activity levels. *Pediatric Exercise Science, 24*, 435–49.

Favazza, P.C., Zeisel, S., Parker, R., & Leboeuf, L. (2011). *Young Athletes Program*. Washington, DC: Special Olympics International.

Klintsova, A. Y., Dickson, E., Yoshida, R., & Greenough, W. T. (2004). Altered expression of BDNF and its high-affinity receptor TrkB in response to complex motor learning and moderate exercise. *Brain Research, 1028,* 92–104.

Ratey, J. J., with Hagerman, E. (2008). *Spark: The revolutionary new science of exercise and the brain.* New York: Little, Brown & Company.

"Target heart rates." (2015). December 12. Retrieved from: www.heart.org

U.S. Department of Health & Human Services. (2008). *Physical activity guidelines for Americans.* Washington, DC: Author.

6

SUPPORTING SOCIAL SKILLS

SELECTION OF TARGET SKILLS

One key advantage of a physical activity program is that it creates natural opportunities for children with ASD to positively interact with their peers with and without disabilities. As discussed in earlier chapters, simply engaging in increased levels of physical activity can have positive impacts in the social domain for children with ASD, and a structured program will provide additional opportunities for positive social interactions.

Recent research indicates that children with ASD may spend as little as 2 percent of their time engaged in social interactions with peers with disabilities (Reszka, Odom, & Hume, 2012) and approximately 8–11 percent of the time engaged in social interactions with typically developing peers (e.g., Tsao et al., 2008) during the school day. Given these low rates of peer engagement, it is crucial that teachers take advantage of opportunities like a structured physical activity program to promote positive peer interactions.

Another consideration is how teachers refer to the physical activity program. This may be especially true for younger children. For example, Burdette and Whitaker (2005) suggest that the language used for the program should focus on the time as "play" rather than use terms such as "physical activity," "exercise," or "sports." This may depend on the children in your classroom, but the program should certainly be fun, and the key is that kids should enjoy being there. This alone will help to encourage positive interactions with peers.

There are a few things teachers can do to determine which social goals to target during a physical activity program. First, it's important for teachers to keep in mind that there will be frequent opportunities for positive social interactions during such a program. Many of the activities you choose will require or embed opportunities for social interactions. You should also continuously look for social opportunities. If you set social interaction as an overall goal of the program, then you can tailor activities or groupings to both maximize and take advantage of these interactions.

Second, use the program time as an opportunity to target existing IEP goals that focus on social interactions. This can be a chance to reinforce existing strategies, and help children generalize their use to new activities and environments. This is also one of the few times during the school day when many teachers are involved in a non-academic activity with the entire class. This makes it an ideal time to target non-academic IEP goals, especially social skills, and to consider how the skills you target connect to activities such as recess or free play. Potential target skills include:

- Initiations
- Responses
- Giving and accepting compliments
    - For example, help kids to attend to their peers during activities. They can cheer on their peers and make specific comments, such as "Nice catch!"
- Taking turns
- Sharing
    - For example, include limited materials in groups so that children need to share.
- Asking for help and helping others
- Including other children in activities

Ideally, the motor skills you teach during the physical activity program will translate to skills needed on the playground or during organized sports, such as maneuvering playground equipment, playing tag, and playing soccer and baseball. In addition, success in the physical activity program should translate into greater confidence in children's ability to "play" with their peers in these activities in other settings. Teachers have observed children interacting or engaging more during recess once they started focusing on motor skills during class. Therefore, this added focus on social skills will support an additional need to help children with ASD join in these activities and stay involved.

Teachers should also consider what type of deficit the targeted social skill represents. Two general ways to view these deficits are as an *acquisition deficit* or as a *performance deficit* (Gresham, Sugai, & Horner, 2001). Acquisition deficits are present if a child is unable to use a skill, or doesn't understand when to use it. Performance deficits occur when a child is able to use a skill, but he or she doesn't use it consistently. Acquisition deficits require direct support in a one-to-one or small-group setting that should most likely occur outside of the physical activity program. Performance deficits are ideal to focus on during the physical activity program, since you know the child is able to perform the skill, and needs to practice it in new settings. Performance deficits are best addressed in the following ways:

- Reinforcing attempts in new environments, such as in the physical activity program or other places, like recess
- Reminding children to use the skill prior to the start of the program each day through supports like Social Stories, Power Cards, and priming
- Utilizing trained peers who encourage and reinforce the behavior

These strategies are discussed late in the chapter.

Third, closely observe your children during the program to better understand what is working well and what requires more support. According to McConnell (2002), behaviors that may interfere with positive social interactions include repetitive behaviors, self-injurious or other challenging behaviors, and limited proximity to peers. Addressing each of these may produce positive effects on peer social interactions.

For example, stereotypical or repetitive behaviors, such as pacing or hand flapping, tend to occur when children with ASD are stressed or overstimulated. If these are occurring at a frequency or intensity that interferes with participation in the program or interactions with peers, then teachers should look at ways to reduce the behavior. This could involve observation and assessment to determine when these behaviors are more or less likely to occur. The key is to reduce the stress or overstimulation, so children with ASD are better able to participate in the program.

Teachers can also adjust the program to include more of the activities that are less stressful for the child with ASD, or provide additional practice in certain activities outside of the program in order to make them more routine. Sometimes children with ASD need more practice to gain confidence, and then they can more easily participate in the program. Teachers could also embed calming activities to help children stabilize their arousal levels.

If interfering behaviors continue, then this may be an ideal time to utilize other staff members, such as a paraprofessional or a behavior specialist. A paraprofessional can provide support with data collection or specific interventions. A behavior specialist can help with the development and implementation of new interventions or supports to address interfering behaviors.

Teachers can use data collection systems, such as an ABC (Antecedent, Behavior, Consequence) form, or observe the class to note common concerns for the whole class, small groups of children, or individual children. As with other academic and behavioral concerns, it makes the most sense to address these concerns using an RTI (Response to Intervention) model whereby the whole class is addressed first. Then work with small groups for children that need additional support. Finally, work individually with children that require the most intensive support.

SUPPORTING SKILLS IN THE CLASSROOM

Teachers can impact social engagement and development during a physical activity program by adjusting the program to encourage or support social interactions, and by providing focused interventions or strategies that facilitate appropriate social interactions.

Environmental Modifications

Environmental modifications involve adjustments that teachers can make to the structure of the program. The idea here is that these changes will create opportunities for success so that children feel more comfortable and are more engaged in the activities. These changes, and other strategies discussed later in the chapter (such as priming), should also reduce stress and anxiety for children with ASD. Then they are more likely to have positive social interactions with peers.

Changes can involve adjustments to the *space* being used, to the *groupings* of children, or to other areas. Ideally, this is done proactively to optimize the program environment. As needs arise, though, it is certainly acceptable to make adjustments during the program. For example, teachers should use a consistent space, if possible, and look for one with limited distractions. In addition, teachers should try to pair children with ASD to work with peers they get along with, and carefully select typically developing peers to serve as both models and partners. Peer-mediated supports that include strategies for training certain peers to work with children with ASD are discussed later in this chapter.

Key areas that may be modified to produce positive effects on peer interactions include having activities that children *prefer*, using materials and activities that are *predictable*, and including activities that are *structured*. These strategies were discussed in detail in chapter 4. At some level, all these areas reduce anxiety for children with ASD so they are more likely to successfully complete activities and have successful interactions with peers. For example, teachers have noticed that children with ASD performed better during the program when activities were repeated. Then as their comfort level increased and they became used to the routine, the children with ASD also began to attend to peers more frequently.

Positive Reinforcement

Increasing the frequency of positive reinforcement can impact behaviors and increase student involvement. A rule of thumb is that teachers should use a five-to-one ratio of positive reinforcement to redirections. Teachers will find the behaviors they reinforce or praise are more likely to occur in the future. This positive feedback will also help children with ASD feel better about themselves, and lead to increased participation in the program.

Praise (or positive reinforcement) can involve simple acts, such as smiles, high fives, or pats on the back. When possible, teachers should also pair this with clear, direct statements that describe what the child did. Such as, "You used your friend's name, Thomas!" or "You shared the ball with José!" This descriptive praise can help lead to increased opportunities for positive peer interactions.

Picture Schedules

Picture schedules were discussed in chapter 4. Detailed visual schedules that help children understand what to expect during the program and provide key ideas for how to perform specific skills can help children engage more appropriately during the program. This will help create opportunities for appropriate peer interactions.

Priming or Previewing

Priming was also discussed in chapter 4. Teachers can use priming as a way to help children engage more appropriately with their peers. One way this works is by reducing the anxiety children with ASD may feel during classroom activities (Grenier & Yeaton, 2011). For example, during a priming session a teacher could remind a child with ASD to engage in specific behaviors during the physical activity program, such as talking to his or her peers or taking turns with peers.

It can also be helpful to remind children to do three things during the physical activity program. Focusing on too many skills or behaviors during a priming session may be overwhelming, but focusing on three provides a manageable number of ideas for kids with ASD to consider during the day's program. In this example, one or two of the suggestions could involve prosocial behaviors, such as practicing responding to peers when they talk to you, or taking turns with peers during a game. The priming session also might be an ideal time to use a Social Story that focuses on social interactions and skills to use during a physical activity program.

Modeling and Role Play

Modeling and role play can also be used to practice specific social skills. This was discussed in detail in chapter 4. Some of the opportunities for practice could occur at a time separate from the physical activity program. This could be a time to focus on skills that you have noticed a child struggling with in a safe environment, either a one-to-one or in a small-group situation. This can be a space where you can help children practice the skills. For example, tell children to stand in their space, such as on a floor marker, and stay one arm's length from peers. Demonstrate and model what this looks like. Teachers should also focus on key ideas like self-esteem and success, so that children are more engaged.

The teacher then can help children to work to generalize these skills to the physical activity program time. You should focus on just one or two skills at a time, such as using a friend's name, taking turns, or sharing. Then provide positive reinforcement for any attempt. Teachers may also want to keep behavior charts, using checkmarks, stickers, or stars, as a way to reinforce positive social behaviors.

Scripts or Cue Cards

Written scripts or cue cards provide a visual, concrete, and portable strategy to teach appropriate conversational skills and behaviors (Ganz, 2007). Scripts are short (three to seven lines) and generally include both a statement and question within each response. The script should be written on the child's reading level, and students should practice it with a parent, teacher, or a peer prior to using it during the program. One rule of thumb could be that a child could practice with the script, practice without the script, and then use the script during the physical activity program. Textbox 6.1 presents suggested steps for implementing a social script.

TEXTBOX 6.1.
Steps for using scripts or cue cards

Step 1: Choose a social skill to target.
Step 2: Observe typically developing children performing the skill.
Step 3: Consider the steps required to successfully complete the skill.
Step 4: Write the script.
Step 5: Teach the script using modeling and guided practice.
Step 6: Use the script during the physical activity program. It may help to have the script on a card.
Step 7: Fade the script.

Teachers should use a script to teach simple social initiation and social response skills, such as "cheering for classmates" or "joining a game." An example script is presented in textbox 6.2.

TEXTBOX 6.2.
Social script: Cheering for classmates

Look around and pay attention to your classmates during an activity or game.

When a classmate catches the ball, say:

Nice catch, _______! (Insert friend's name)

When a classmate makes a good throw, say:

Great throw, _______! (Insert friend's name)

Any time a classmate does something well, or if others are cheering for him or her, say:

Awesome job, _______! (Insert friend's name)

Social Narratives

Social narratives attempt to describe as situation, the perspectives of those involved, and the behavioral expectations (Wong et al., 2013). One type of social narrative is a Social Story. Social Stories try to describe the situation in which a behavior will occur, describe the perspectives of those involved, and provide suggestions for what the child can do in the future.

Gray (2004) outlined the specific details for writing stories, but the research has not proven that her formula and criteria are required. Basically, she outlined use of different sentence types, such as descriptive, perspective, and directive. In general, teachers should try to write stories that describe more than they direct. In other words, help explain the situation to children, including how people feel and their perspectives (e.g., "My teacher likes it when I stand quietly on my floor marker and wait for directions, because this helps me know what we are doing in the activity").

The phrasing directs the child to *stand quietly on his floor marker*, but clearly explains why this is important. Some stories may include pictures or illustrations. This doesn't seem to be required, but can help illustrate the expectations. It may help to have the child draw his or her own pictures. This way the teacher is sure the child understands the expectations, and therefore may be more likely to engage in the expected behavior.

Based on existing research, some components seem to improve outcomes when using Social Stories or a social narrative. These include:

- Getting input from the child with ASD
- Focusing on a limited number of specific behaviors
- Writing on the student's receptive level
- Reading the story immediately (or as close as possible) before the program
- Including comprehension questions to help ensure the child understands expectations and alternative behaviors
- Involving families and other school personnel, when possible (Denning, 2007).

See textbox 6.3 for a sample social narrative on working with partners.

TEXTBOX 6.3.
Social narrative: Playing catch

Sometimes we play games in school. One game is playing catch. During catch, we take turns throwing the ball back and forth. We can use any type of ball, such as a tennis ball, baseball, basketball, or football. I should try to throw the ball so it hits my partner in the hands. If I don't, it's ok. I'll try again the next time.

When my partner makes a good throw or catch, I can say, "Great catch!" or "Nice throw!" This will make my partner feel happy.

Playing catch is fun. When the teacher tells us the game is over, we can get ready for the next game.

Peer-Mediated Interventions

Children with ASD are more likely to interact with adults than with their peers in the classroom (e.g., Brown, Odom, Li, & Zercher, 1999). One reason is they are more likely to receive a positive response from an adult, and therefore try to continue that interaction, rather than attempt an interaction with a peer (Harper & McCluskey, 2003). One way to counteract this pattern and to take advantage of engaged peers in the classroom is to use peer-mediated interventions. Peer involvement can support the use of both appropriate motor and social skills. Use of trained peers in the classroom activities has been very effective (e.g., Watkins et al., 2014).

Pivotal response training (PRT) involves targeting "pivotal" areas of development, such as motivation, responses to multiple cues, self-management, and initiations (Koegel & Koegel, 2006). The idea is that improvements in these pivotal areas will impact broader areas, such as sociability, communication, and behavior. One way to use PRT during the program is to combine it with peer training. Harper and colleagues (2008) did a study that trained peers to work with target children with ASD during recess.

In this way, peers can be trained to target specific skills in a small-group setting when they are paired with classmates with ASD. Key areas to target would include gaining attention, narrating activities, reinforcing attempts, and taking turns. These strategies may work best if the child with ASD receives support prior to the peer interactions and are taught using key words, such as *look* and *listen*, that peers will use as they try to gain the child's attention.

- Gaining attention: Peers should be taught to get the attention of the child with ASD before offering him or her a choice in the activity or providing directions. Peers should be encouraged to use the child's name and to make eye contact. They can also prompt the child with ASD to *look* and *listen* to them.
- Narrating activities: Peers should be taught to model their completion of the activities and narrate what they are doing. For example, they could show examples of activities (e.g., "Look, let's use the ball to play catch") or describe what they are doing with materials (e.g., "Here, I'll throw the ball to you and you throw it back" or "Catch the ball like this"). Peers will also need to match their language with the target child's receptive language abilities. Therefore, some language may need to be simplified (e.g., "Let's play catch" or "Catch the ball," then "throw the ball").
- Reinforcing attempts: Peers should be taught to enthusiastically praise the child with ASD for any attempts to participate and complete the skills. This can include high-fives, thumbs-up gestures, and big smiles, and verbal praise like "Great catch!" "Now you do it!" or "High five!"
- Taking turns: Peers should be taught to work on taking turns. Peers should offer turns with materials and equipment, or show the child with ASD how he or she can share common items.

Teachers should include key ideas in the training sessions. These include supporting peer helpers using verbal explanations, modeling, role playing, feedback, visual supports, and prompting (Watkins et al., 2014).

TAKEAWAYS

1. Physical activity programs create natural opportunities for children with ASD to have positive interactions with peers.
2. Careful consideration of target skills will help teachers identify target skills and consider which can be supported during the program.
3. The first step involves adjusting the environment to support positive peer interactions.
4. The teachers can selectively choose additional support strategies.

REFERENCES

Brown, W., Odom, S., Li, S., & Zercher, C. (1999). Ecobehavioral assessment in early childhood programs: A portrait of preschool inclusion. *Journal of Special Education, 33*, 138–53.

Burdette, H. L., & Whitaker, R. C. (2005). Resurrecting free play in young children: Looking beyond fitness and fatness to attention, affiliation, and affect. *Archives of Pediatrics and Adolescent Medicine 159*, 46–50.

Denning, C. B. (2007). Social skills interventions for students with Asperger syndrome and high functioning autism: Research findings and implications for teachers. *Beyond Behavior, 16,* 16–23.

Ganz, J. B. (2007). Using visual script interventions to address communication skills. *Teaching Exceptional Children, 40*(2), 54–58.

Gray, C. (2004). Social Stories 10.0: The new defining criteria and guidelines. *Jenison Autism Journal, 15,* 2–21.

Grenier, M., & Yeaton, P. (2011). Previewing: A successful strategy for students with autism. *Journal of Physical Education, Recreation, and Dance, 82*(1), 28–43.

Gresham, F. M., Sugai, G., & Horner, R. H. (2001). Interpreting outcomes of social skills training for students with high-incidence disabilities. *Exceptional Children, 67*(3), 331–44.

Harper, C. B., Symon, J. B. G., & Frea, W. D. (2008). Recess is time-in: Using peers to improve social skills of children with autism. *Journal of Autism and Developmental Disorders, 38*, 815–26.

Harper, L. V., & McCluskey, K. S. (2003). Teacher-child and child-child interactions in inclusive preschool settings: Do adults inhibit peer interactions? *Early Childhood Research Quarterly, 18*, 163–84.

Koegel, R. L., & Koegel, L. K. (2006). *Pivotal response treatments for autism: Communication, social, & academic development.* Baltimore, MD: Brookes.

McConnell, S. R. (2002). Interventions to facilitate social interaction for young children with autism: Review of available research and recommendations for educational intervention and future research. *Journal of Autism and Developmental Disorders, 32*(5), 351–72.

Reszka, S. S., Odom, S. L., & Hume, K. A. (2012). Ecological features of preschools and the social engagement of children with autism. *Journal of Early Intervention, 34*, 40–56.

Tsao, L., Odom, S., Buysse, V., Skinner, M., West, T., & Vitztum-Komanecki, J. (2008). Social participation of children with disabilities in inclusive preschool programs: Program typology and ecological features. *Exceptionality, 16*, 125–40.

Watkins, L., O'Reilly, M., Kuhn, M., Gevarter, C., Lancioni, G. E., Sigafoos, J., & Lang, R. (2014). A review of peer-mediated social interaction interventions for students with autism in inclusive settings. *Journal of Autism and Developmental Disabilities, 45*(4), 1070–83.

Wong, C., Odom, S. L., Hume, K. Cox, A. W., Fettig, A., Kucharczyk, S., et al. (2013). *Evidence-based practices for children, youth, and young adults with Autism Spectrum Disorder.* Chapel Hill: Frank Porter Graham Child Development Institute, Autism Evidence-Based Practice Review Group, University of North Carolina.

7

COLLABORATIONS

The classroom teacher's job is increasingly demanding. It is therefore crucial that teachers build effective collaborations with home and related service personnel (e.g., Friend & Cook, 2010). This chapter will highlight strategies to collaborate with families and other school personnel (e.g., physical education teachers, occupational therapists) in order to support motor development and movement throughout the school day, and to ensure that skills are practiced across contexts.

COLLABORATING WITH FAMILIES

Support

Supporting families is crucial for the development of successful classroom programs, and sets the stage for collaboration. Just getting some families involved in class activities will be a process. Teachers should work to build relationships, develop shared goals and decision making, and promote active communication with families (Friend & Cook, 2010). Support involves a number of important skills, including being empathetic to the stress that many families experience, listening, and showing respect for the family.

It may be particularly difficult for some families to get involved with the program in the school. Therefore, teachers should start early in the year and encourage involvement. Be as flexible as possible about ways family members can get involved and times for them to come to school to observe the program. Finally, focus on the positives for all your students.

Communication

Create lines of communication with families early in the school year. Try to establish the best way to communicate with families by offering choices that include email, texts, text alerts, phone calls, or notes home. Create regularly scheduled meetings that are face to face, online, or in person (Mueller, Singer, & Draper, 2008). Encourage families to come in to see what is happening in the classroom. Some families may enjoy observing during the physical activity program, since it is more active and highly reinforcing for the kids. Teachers can also send home materials related to the physical activity program in order to get families more involved. This can also include sharing outcomes for children and involving the program in the IEP goal development. Both of these ideas are expanded on below.

Participation

Once family members hear about the physical activity program or see it in action, they may be more willing to participate in some way. Highlight the potential benefits for children in the program. These include opportunities for movement, learning new motor skills, experiencing success in the classroom, and positive interactions with peers and adults. Participation may also lead to health benefits and the potential for a lifestyle change that could impact concerns such as obesity. Lastly, children may learn new skills that could help create opportunities outside of school, such as playing on the playground, in their neighborhood, or through organized sports.

If family members are able to come to the school to provide support with the program, teachers should assign them specific jobs. For example, have them work with children at a station focusing on a specific motor skill, or follow a group to help keep them on track. Try to keep the expectations clear and simple.

Interventions are more effective when children can practice skills at home with parents or siblings (Zhang & Wheeler, 2011). For example, inform families about the skill focus for each week. The hope is that families will be more likely to practice and reinforce these skills at home once they have learned about them in your classroom.

Feedback

Help parents understand the benefits of engaging in the physical activity program. This can be accomplished by sharing outcome data on children or weekly reports on the progress children have made. Some outcomes can also be connected to IEP goals.

IEP Goals

Consider how skills addressed during the physical activity program may be connected to existing IEP goals for children. Table 7.1 lists potential goals

Table 7.1. Potential connections with IEP goals

Goal Area	*Sample Focus Goals*
Readiness skills/ self-regulation	• Wait for turn patiently • Transition between activities • Follow oral and written directions • Participate in group activities • Attempt new activities or tasks • Listen when others are speaking • Request clarification when necessary • Complete requested action • Follow one-step, two-step, or three-step directions
Motor skills	• Improve gross motor skills • Perform age-appropriate gross motor activities and exercise • Cross the midline during task performance • Track visual objects • Plan actions before carrying them out • Identify directionality words (e.g., left, right, forward, backward, up, down) • Develop hand preference for tasks • Improve overall body strength • Improve physical endurance
Social skills (communication)	• Take turns • Share with others • Maintain eye contact during conversations • Engage in verbal compliments • Accept assistance • Support others in need of help • Play cooperatively with at least one other peer

that could be addressed during the physical activity program in three general areas: readiness skills and self-regulation, motor skills, and social skills. Many skills are intertwined with participation in a physical activity program.

COLLABORATING WITH OTHER PROFESSIONALS

Interventions have been found to be more effective when collaboration occurred across school staff (Zhang & Wheeler, 2011). School staff can also collaborate to focus on teaching strategies, behavioral supports, and ways to create fun and engaging activities that keep kids actively involved (Murata & Tan, 2009).

Physical Education Teachers

Seek out physical education (PE) or adapted physical education (APE) teachers as the experts on motor development, exercise, and physical activity. If you're feeling unsure about how to deliver certain aspects of the physical activity program, then collaborating with the PE or APE teacher can help target certain areas, such as finding appropriate exercise activities or learning how to perform specific motor skills. These teachers can help you improve and adjust aspects of the physical activity program (Klein & Hollingshead, 2015). They may be able to provide suggestions for individualizing or differentiating aspects of the physical activity program for specific children. It may also be helpful to get more involved in the physical education classes with your students. This can improve relationships and create opportunities for further collaborations. Lastly, collaborating with a PE teacher on the development of the IEP could improve student outcomes and lead to shared goals (Kowalski, Lieberman, & Daggett, 2006). This may also have the added benefit of helping children experience greater success in PE class through shared goals, and a deeper understanding of children's needs.

Occupational Therapists

Occupational therapists (OTs) or physical therapists (PTs) can provide expertise on fine and gross motor skill development. Children must qualify for services from either an OT or PT, based upon assessment results and the impact of their disability on school performance. If a child qualifies, then some of their IEP goals may be tied to physical activity and gross motor development. If a child doesn't qualify, the specialist may still be willing to consult with you on ideas for the program. OTs and PTs get very excited when teachers want to focus on motor development and movement in their classrooms. They can be very helpful as you consider activities that target specific motor skills or differentiate activities for certain children. They may also be able to help you consider new ways to adapt different materials to meet the needs of everyone in your classroom.

Paraprofessionals

Develop a clear plan with support staff in your classroom during the physical activity program. This can include involving support staff in the process of developing the program and planning daily lessons. Create clear roles and expectations throughout the program. Provide times for practicing activities. Roles that paraprofessionals can take on include data collection, working one-on-one or in small groups, or leading stations during motor development activities. One support to consider is the use of performance feedback for paraprofessionals (Rispoli, Neely, Lang, & Ganz, 2011). This could include training prior to starting the program, and daily feedback following the program. This feedback can help everyone stay on the same page and determine the best practices to use during the program each day. In general, keep feedback positive and consistent.

TAKEAWAYS

1. Collaborating with colleagues and families during the development and implementation of the physical activity program will improve outcomes for children.
2. Create time in your schedule for planning across team members.
3. Use the physical activity program to focus on IEP goals.

REFERENCES

Friend, M., & Cook, L. (2010). *Interactions: Collaboration skills for school professionals* (6th ed.). Columbus, OH: Merrill.

Klein, E., & Hollingshead, A. (2015). Collaboration between special and physical education: The benefits of a healthy lifestyle for all students. *Teaching Exceptional Children, 47*(3), 163–71. doi:10.1177/0040059914558945

Kowalski, E., Lieberman, M., & Daggett, S. (2006). Getting involved in the IEP process. *Journal of Physical Education, Recreation, and Dance, 77*(7), 35–39. doi:10.1080/07303084.2006.10597905

Mueller, T., Singer, G., & Draper, L. (2008). Reducing parental dissatisfaction with special education in two school districts: Implementing conflict prevention and alternative dispute resolution. *Journal of Educational and Psychological Consultation, 18*, 191–233.

Murata, N., & Tan, C. (2009). Collaborative teaching of motor skills for preschoolers with developmental delays. *Early Childhood Education Journal, 36*, 483–89. doi:10.1007/s10643-007-0212-5

Rispoli, M., Neely, L., Lang, R., & Ganz, J. (2011). Training paraprofessionals to implement interventions for people with autism spectrum disorders: A systematic review. *Developmental Neurorehabilitation, 14*(6), 378–88.

Zhang, J., & Wheeler, J. J. (2011). A meta-analysis of peer-mediated interventions for young children with autism spectrum disorders. *Education and Training in Autism and Developmental Disorders, 46*(1), 62–77.

Lightning Source UK Ltd.
Milton Keynes UK
UKHW01f0335190618
324453UK00001B/32/P

9 781475 817652